WORSHIP NOW

Worship Now

A Collection of Services and Prayers for Public Worship

Compiled by
David Cairns
Ian Pitt-Watson
James A. Whyte
T. B. Honeyman

Edinburgh
THE SAINT ANDREW PRESS

© The Saint Andrew Press 1972
First published in 1972 by
The Saint Andrew Press,
121 George Street, Edinburgh, EH2 4YN

ISBN 0 7152 0199 9

Printed in Great Britain by
R. & R. CLARK, LTD.,
Brandon Street, Edinburgh

CONTENTS

		page
INTRODUCTION		vii
ACKNOWLEDGEMENTS		ix

SECTION A
Prayers for Morning Worship   1

SECTION B
Sacraments and Ordinances
1. Sacraments of Baptism — First Order   34
2.   — Second Order   37
3.   — Third Order   40
4. Admission to First Communion   42
5. Service of Confirmation   44
6. Holy Communion — First Order   47
7.   — Second Order   53
8.   — Third Order   57
9. Short Order for Holy Communion   61
10. Folk Communion   64
11. A House Communion   68
12. Marriage Service — First Order   70
13.   — Second Order   76
14.   — Third Order   80
15. Funeral Service — First Order   86
16.   — Second Order   88
17. Service for the Crematorium — First Order   93
18.   — Second Order   96

SECTION C
New Forms of Worship
1. Family Worship, Sunday before Christmas   100
2. Order for Evening Service   107
3. Family Service   111
4. Meditation on Ask, Seek, Knock   115
5. Morning Prayers   118
6. Services on Special Themes — The Individual   119
    — Disability   121
7. A Small Communion   124
8. A Dance Drama of the Holy Spirit   132

v

CONTENTS

SECTION D

The Christian Year and Occasional Services   page
1. Four Prayers for Advent   137
2. The Second Sunday in Advent (Bible Sunday)   141
3. A Christmas Eve Service   143
4. A Christmas Eve Service   148
5. Christmas Family Service   152
6. The Last Sunday of the Year   157
7. The First Sunday of the Year   158
8. The Passion of our Lord   159
9. Three Hour Service, Good Friday   164
10. An Easter Eucharist   166
11. Pentecost Intercession   175
12. After Pentecost   177
13. Prayers for All Saints   179
14. Prayers for Civic Occasions   182
15. Kirking of the Council   187
16. Youth Service   190
17. Harvest Thanksgiving   192

SECTION E

An Anthology of Prayers and Introductory Sentences
1. Sentences Introducing Worship   198
2. Contact   202
3. Prayers for Adoration   203
4. Adoration and Meditation   205
5. A Prayer of Approach   206
6. For Renewal of the Church   208
7. For Unity   208
8. Except the Lord Build the House   209
9. General Prayer   210
10. Liturgy of Intercession   211
11. Thanksgiving by Affluent Christians   212
12. The Ministry of Reconciliation   213
13. Following a Road Accident   214
14. Christmas   215
15. For a Funeral Service   216
16. After the Lesson at a Funeral   216
17. Ordination   218
18. For the people we meet   219
19. Abundant Life   219
20. When there is a Strike   220
21. Evening   220

INTRODUCTION

It is just over two years since the suggestion was made that an informal group of members of the Church of Scotland should collect in a book some material for Church Prayers and Services, following the lead that had been so effectively given in England by Caryl Micklem and his friends. We wondered at first whether we should not here follow the principle that what the Churches can do together in good conscience, they should not try to do apart. We wondered, that is, whether we should not invite our Scottish friends in other Churches to come in with us on this project. But on second thoughts, though no scruples of conscience held us back from such cooperation, we felt that the traditions of worship were rather different, and that in a temporary production like this book we would do well to confine ourselves to what was happening in the Church of Scotland.

We had become aware that there was very little knowledge in one congregation of what was being done in the field of worship in other places, and we were convinced that it would be a great help and encouragement if recent experience were shared, both in relation to 'middle of the road' services, and in relation to more original types of prayer and service.

We wish to explain that our method of collection of material has not been systematic; the idea of the book in the first instance came from a group of friends, and from their friends. This is not to say that it represents any one viewpoint on theological or liturgical matters. Those who are on the look-out for discrepancies will find contributions which are not in theological agreement with others. From this it must be seen that as compilers we do not accept theological responsibility for the contributions, although sometimes we have asked an author to accept slight changes which we thought from a linguistic point of view would sound better, or from a theological point of view would be more satisfactory. We would welcome further contributions from anyone for a possible second volume, if the need for one becomes evident.

Thus our book is not fully representative of the best that is being produced in our Church, nor is it comprehensive in the selection of themes. What we have printed has necessarily been dictated by what was sent to us. When we have asked people to write for us prayers on a theme which appeared to have been omitted, it has not always been possible to secure from busy men what we asked for, and we have tried to avoid delays such as would be inevitable if we were to commission prayers or services, and then wait until they were sent us. Our book is fragmentary, and, indeed, fugitive, and we are content that it should be so.

We have been greatly encouraged by the all but universal welcome that our project has received, even from those who did not feel that they had anything at the moment to give us. We are still more grateful to those who took great trouble to submit material for our consideration, modestly saying that they were glad to help us, but did not mind if their work did not find a place in the book.

But our idea in compiling the book has not been merely to give information. We wish to stimulate and encourage those who feel the need to create new forms of prayer, or to revise old ones. An unofficial book does not require to have the balance and careful composition expected of an official Book of Common Order. It can, therefore, be produced more quickly in response to a need, as it may be the more quickly superseded. Yet we have reason to believe that what our contributors have given us may not be without use in preparing the way for a new official Book of Common Order which will have a much more lasting value and authoritative character.

The division of the book into five parts according to the nature of the services is to some extent arbitrary, and it was not always easy to say under which category an item should be included.

March, 1972

ACKNOWLEDGEMENTS

In the construction of prayers and services, the writer will often be influenced by others who have trodden the same paths before. Therefore we must make general acknowledgement to similar publications, old and new, which have influenced to a greater or lesser degree what is contained in this book.

More specifically, the publishers acknowledge their indebtedness to the following for permission to quote from copyright material:

Biblical passages:

New English Bible, second edition, © 1970 used by permission of Oxford and Cambridge University Presses;

The Revised Standard Version of the Bible, © 1946 and 1952 and used by permission;

The Jerusalem Bible © 1966, 1967 and 1968 by Darton, Longman and Todd Ltd. and Doubleday and Company Inc., used by permission;

S.C.M. Press Ltd., for the Communion Service by Professor Barclay published in *The Lord's Supper,* and for the adaptation of a prayer for a Cremation Service from *Contemporary Prayers for Public Worship* edited by Caryl Micklem;

Hodder and Stoughton Ltd., for the adaptation of a prayer from *Parish Prayers* edited by Frank Colquhoun;

Epworth Press, for a quotation from *The Promise of the Spirit* by William Barclay.

SECTION A
Prayers for Morning Service

1

(A) 2015
adopted.

Let us worship God

God is light, and in him there is no darkness at all.
Only the man who loves his brother dwells in light.

Let us sing to God's Praise   (*A hymn of praise*)

Let us pray:
God our Father, you have made the light shine out of darkness; you have made the sun rise (on the good and on the evil)
You have given Jesus Christ to be the light of the world.
Today you have awakened us and brought us here to praise
your goodness and to ask for your blessing. We turn our
thoughts towards you; we lift our minds to think of you;
and though we cannot see you because you live in light
inaccessible hid from our eyes, yet we know that you are
present in power and love to receive our praises and to give
your help and strength, through Jesus Christ our Lord.

Gracious Father, we know that all our failures and short-
comings stand revealed in the clear light of your goodness.
We ask your forgiveness. Forgive our hardness of heart and
impenitence of spirit; our pride, self-sufficiency, and
wilful wrongdoing. Forgive our readiness to blame, and our
want of thoughtfulness, patience, kindness, and sympathy
in our dealings with others. Forgive our every failure to
let the mind of Christ be formed in us, and to choose the
path of service which he set before us.

> Lord, have mercy upon us.
> *Christ, have mercy upon us.*
> Lord, have mercy upon us.

Be assured, there is declared in Jesus Christ to all
who are truly penitent, the forgiveness of their sins, for
his Name's sake.

Set before our hearts and minds each day, Lord God, the
example of Jesus Christ. Help us to love as he loved; help
us to live as he lived; help us to be neighbours to our
fellow men in their need as he in his mercy was neighbour
to us, and suffered and died for us. In his light may we go
to our work; in his strength may we live this week; in his
service may our lives be spent; and may his will be always
done; and to him, with you, our Father, and the Holy Spirit,
be the glory and the praise, now and always.   AMEN

Old Testament Lesson

Metrical Psalm

New Testament Lesson: Epistle:
Gospel:

(*The response to the bidding* 'Let us pray to the Lord'
is '*Lord, hear our prayer*'.)

For Christian people in every place, that they may shine
as lights in a dark world: let us pray to the Lord:
Lord, hear our prayer.

For the congregation of this church — for men and women and
children, that they may be faithful followers of Jesus
Christ: let us pray to the Lord:

For our Queen and her Prime Minister and Government, and for
our leaders, that we may be ruled wisely and well:
let us pray . . . . . .

For all whose work helps us day by day — for those who serve
us in shops, for those who clean our streets, for policemen
who keep the peace, that they may find happiness in helping
others: let us pray . . . . . .

For those who are ill, especially any whom we know and name
now in silence . . . . . .; and for those who care for them —

2

relatives, doctors and nurses, that Jesus' work of healing may continue in our day: let us pray . . . . . .

For our homes; for parents, brothers and sisters, sons and daughters, and for all who are dear to us that they may know that all are the children of our one God and Father: let us pray . . . . . .

For any others whom we ought to remember, and for any who have asked for our prayers . . . . . .: let us pray . . . . . .

All these, our prayers, we offer in the name and for the sake of Jesus Christ our Lord who lives and reigns with you, O Father, and the Holy Spirit, one God, world without end.   AMEN

Hymn

Words of Authority — SERMON — Ascription of Glory

Offerings uplifted

Proclamations and Intimations

(*Offerings brought forward while an offering verse is sung*)

(Lift up your hearts!
We lift them up unto the Lord.
Let us give thanks to our Lord God.
It is meet and right so to do.)

Truly it is good for us to thank you, heavenly Father, for the wealth and beauty of the world in which we live, and for all the variety of the human race. We thank you for all that comes to us through the skill, labour and love of other people, and are glad that our experience is enriched by men and women from every walk of life, of every colour, language and belief. Most of all we thank you for the new light shed upon life by Jesus, whom you appointed to be our example, our teacher and our Saviour. (With his faithful followers throughout the world, and with the unseen heavenly hosts, we join to praise you in the everlasting hymn:

Holy, holy, holy, Lord God of hosts,
heaven and earth are full of your glory.
Glory be to you, O Lord most high.)

And now, most merciful Father, we humbly pray you,
through Jesus Christ, your Son, our Lord, to receive and
bless the offering of our worship and our gifts, and so to
consecrate our bodies, minds and spirits by the operation
of your Holy Spirit, the Lord, and giver of life, that we
may give ourselves to you, a living sacrifice, dedicated
and fit for your acceptance, for such is the worship which
we, as rational creatures, should offer . . . . . . through
Jesus Christ our Lord.

Finally we pray you to bring us, O Lord God, at our last
awakening into the house and gate of heaven, to enter into
that gate and dwell in that house, where there shall be no
darkness nor dazzling, but one equal light; no noise nor
silence, but one equal music; no fears nor hopes, but one
equal possession; no ends nor beginnings, but one equal
eternity; in the habitations of your glory and dominion,
world without end; And now as our Saviour Christ has taught
us we are bold to say:
OUR FATHER . . . . . .

Hymn

Benediction

Dispersal verse

2

A Psalm of Praise

Jesus said: 'Be careful not to make a show of your religion before men: if you do, no reward awaits you in your Father's house in heaven.

'And if you greet your brothers, what is there extraordinary about that? Even the heathen do as much. You must therefore be all goodness, just as your heavenly Father is all good.'

Let us pray:
O God, our heavenly Father, the source from whom we come and the end to whom we travel, help us to worship with reverence and with sincerity. Quieten our restless minds, strengthen our uncertain faith, stir our sleeping consciences.

O Lord our King, we have been given our lives with their richness of opportunity and their wealth of interest, but too often we have wasted and misused them. We complain and grumble, forgetting what others endure cheerfully. We are hard on our neighbours and generous to ourselves. We keep wearing the blinkers of prejudice, because the light of truth hurts us. We can be boastful and conceited, rude and selfish, quick to take offence, sure that we are right and that others are wrong.

O Lord Jesus, the real light of the world, show us what we are like, and make us truly sorry.

And may God grant to all who are penitent the assurance that their sins are forgiven, and the blessing of his peace.

Almighty God, without whom we are weak and helpless, be with us in our daily lives.

We pray for faith; for faith in the creative Love by whom the world was made; for faith in the divine purpose and action shown to us in Jesus Christ; for faith in his Church which the forces of death shall never overpower.

Lord, give us faith.

We pray for hope; for hope that good will triumph over evil, truth over falsehood, beauty over ugliness; for hope that men will never think themselves too strong to depend on God; for hope that our present trials are the birth-pangs of a new and better order.

Lord, give us hope.

We pray for love; for the love which is very patient, very kind; for the love which delights in the truth; for the love which has no limits to its faith, its hope, its endurance.

Lord, give us love.

The Lord's Prayer

Hymn:

Old Testament Lesson

The Epistle

Hymn:

The Gospel

The Apostles' Creed (R.C.H. 724)

The Anthem

Thanksgiving and Intercession

Let us pray:
O Lord our God, teach us to be more truly thankful. May we never take for granted all that makes life rich and full. We give thanks for its interest and variety, for everything that stimulates and enriches our minds; for our pleasures and recreations; for our standard of living and the comfort of our homes; for the advance of medical skill which keeps us healthy.

We give thanks for the Christian faith which is our heritage, for the values which underpin and permeate our national life; for the Church of Jesus Christ and his constant presence with it; for the growth of understanding between Christians, for the breaking down of old barriers and the birth of a new tolerance.

We give thanks for Jesus himself; for his hatred of sin
and his love for sinners; for his compassion and his teaching; for the fullness of life we see in him, and for the light
of the knowledge of thy glory in his face.

Hear our prayers of intercession.

We pray for the peace and unity of the Church. May
Christians work together as salt and leaven in the world,
bring truth and integrity into the life of individuals and
nations. May their whole concern be for Christ to be seen in
and through all that they do in their separate communions.
May their love and devotion to him be the flame which welds
them together.

We pray for our beloved country. Bless and guide our
sovereign lady the Queen, Prince Philip and all the members
of the Royal House. Give courage and wisdom to our
ministers of state, to business and trade union leaders and
to all in positions of responsibility. Help us all to see
our part in the divine plan, to give our best in working
not just for ourselves but for the whole community, and to
learn from our experience, with courage and with hope.

Lord, bring peace to this troubled world. Give sanity to
us all, that we may stop building up weapons of war and
begin to use our science and technology to feed the hungry
and to help the underprivileged to help themselves.

Keep us sensitive to the needs of the poor, the unemployed, the helpless, the refugees and the stateless.
And may our sympathy show itself not in words only but in
action.

We remember all who have great power and influence,
scientists, business magnates, journalists, playwrights,
film and television directors and entertainers, that they
may use their talents for good.

We pray for young people in trouble and for all who work
with them, especially social workers, borstal and prison
officers.

We remember those in distress of mind or body; the sick, and those who suffer from nervous depression or sleeplessness ; the bereaved and the lonely; the handicapped and the old; and especially any whom we know and name in the silence . . . . . .

O God of our fathers, the God not of the dead but of the living, we give praise and thanks for all who have gone before us in the faith and of whom we have good hope that they live on with thee. May we follow Jesus as they did, and, when our time comes, pass through the gate of death into the fullnes of life eternal. AMEN

Hymn:

Let us pray:
O God of peace, thou true light of faithful souls and perfect brightness of thy saints, be present to us thy children who now look up to thee.
Give us grace to praise and serve thee as we ought; and grant that the souls which thirst for thy promises may be filled from thine abundance; through Jesus Christ our Lord.

The Sermon

Ascription
And now to God the Father, God the Son and God the Holy Ghost, be ascribed all might, and majesty, dominion and power, both now and for evermore.

The Offering

O Lord our Governor, who art King of all the earth, accept of thine infinite goodness the offerings of thy people which now they yield and dedicate to thee, praying that the same may be used for the extension of thy Church and Kingdom; through Jesus Christ our Lord.

Hymn:

The Benediction

8

3

ON THE THEME OF INDUSTRY
Let us worship God: Let us sing the hymn 'Behold us Lord . . . . . .'
(R.C.H. 242, vv 1-5)

Jesus said: 'Happy are the eyes that see what you see, for
I tell you that many prophets and kings have wanted to see
what you see and never saw it, and to hear what you hear and
never heard it.'

Let us pray:
O God our Father, we meet here this day in the name of Jesus —
because we are glad to be alive. We are glad that our eyes
can see the wonder and beauty of your world and our ears
hear what you are doing in it.

You have awakened us this day, once again, to the love of our
families and friends, which we see and gladly acknowledge.
You uphold us this day, as always, by the service of our
neighbours and the mercies of our fellowmen, which we so
often forget.

You come to us with gifts new every morning; of sun and wind,
of food and shelter, of love and joy and life.

You speak to us also in judgement. We know evil in our own
lives. We see greater suffering in others than we ourselves
could bear. We hear of terrible things in your world. We know
that as men we have failed. We have brought suffering on ourselves and on others.

But your mercies are not withdrawn. Love is renewed. Life
goes on. And we know your forgiveness.

It is Jesus who has given us eyes to see and ears to hear. So
above all else we thank you for him. In him we see our failures
for they nailed him to the Cross. In him we know that love
conquers and that hope endures, because in him we know that
you are at work in the world, whatever we do.

Jesus, you tell us to ask and to seek and to knock.
You promise us that if we do, we'll receive and we'll find,
and doors will open for us.

We confess that we have not asked enough because we prefer
grumbling to receiving.

We have not sought with eagerness because we're afraid of what
we might find.

We have scarcely knocked at all because we know that an open
door would lead us into the unknown.

Especially we confess that in our life together in your
church we have not asked the questions men are asking.

We have not wanted to join with others in their search.

We have been suspicious of doors that, opened, would make us
join with others in their life.

O God, we confess that often we have thought we could see
nothing in the world to make us happy. We have felt that we
were right to be miserable and in despair.

We have been more ready to complain at our lot than to
rejoice in your gifts.

In Jesus you have given us light, but we have stumbled in our
own shadows.

In Jesus you have given us power, but all we can do is to
confess our own weakness.

In Jesus you have given us peace, but we have been anxious
about many things.

In Jesus you have called us into life and we have been afraid.

Forgive us. We are weary of our failures. We are ashamed of
our excuses.

Forgive our forgetfulness of you and of our fellowmen; our
disregard of your kingdom, your power and your glory.

O Lord, you are at this time leading men into new ways.
Give us

> a new mind to understand your loving purposes,
> a new heart to rejoice in them,
> and a new perseverance to follow the way of Jesus,
> your Son, our brother, to whom be glory for ever.

Let us read two short passages from John's Gospel,
First in chapter 5, verses 8 to 17. I read from
the New English Bible, and then in chapter 9,
verses 1 to 7.

Let us now give thanks for what we have been given to see.
Let us sing the hymn 'Mine eyes have seen the glory of the
coming of the Lord.' (R.C.H. 155)

Sermon

Let us sing the First Hymn in the First Book of Dunblane
Praises; 'Lord, look upon our working days.'

Let us pray
O God, we give thanks for all your goodness to us; for your
goodness to us in our life together with other men; for our
dependence on each other for all that we want in life; for
the enrichment of life that comes to each one of us through
the joy, the achievements, the friendship of other people.

We thank you for the hope of still better things that life
will bring to us when we share with all other men. We thank
you for impatience and frustration with things as they are.
We thank you for the will to struggle and the vision of glory
for all men on earth.

We thank you even for our failures; for the failure of our
selfish hopes, for the suffering that comes through our
blindness, for the knowledge of the cost of our selfishness.

Above all we thank you for Jesus, your Son, our brother, for
the work that he did as carpenter, as teacher, as healer, as
man: for his showing to us of your work in the world: for his
victory of life over death: for the life that is ours even
now in him; for the more abundant life to which he calls us
and all men.

And in his name we pray for them; for all men and women in
their daily work; for all who co-operate with you in the
providing of our daily bread. We pray that they may bear with
patience our inability to share the products of their work.

11

Strengthen in them and in us our commitment to the hope that the day may soon come when men shall share their bread in plenty and in peace.

In particular we pray for all men and women who seek to find the way to new life among men and nations;

> For scientists seeking to find the way to plenty,
> For politicians seeking to find the way to peace,
> For young people seeking to find the way to a fuller life,
> And for all men and women and children in their homes that we may be always seeking and always finding.

And, in love and duty bound, we pray for those who this day suffer through the blindness, the greed, the cruelty of their fellowmen; especially those suffering from the cruelty of war, those suffering from famine, and all, in any land, who suffer from the oppression of their fellows.

Let us pray for our country — for the Queen, her ministers, and all who govern this land, that they may be upheld in their ambition to find a way of justice and peace for all.
In the silence of our hearts we pray for those known to ourselves to be in special need; those who are sick, those who mourn, any who are lonely or anxious or under heavy responsibility.
Bless them and keep them, and cause your face to shine upon them today and for ever . . . . . .

Let us sing in Metrical Psalm no. 145, verses 9-16:
'Good unto all men is the Lord.'

The grace of our Lord Jesus Christ and the love of God and the fellowship of the Holy Spirit be with you all now and evermore.   AMEN

4

· *Sentences:*
Jesus said, 'If you dwell within the revelation I have brought,
you are indeed my disciples; you shall know the truth, and the
truth will set you free.'
Paul said, 'Christ set us free, to be free men, stand firm,
then, and refuse to be tied to the yoke of slavery again.'

Prayer (1)
O God, the Father of all men, as we come together this morning
in your presence, we remember that you want all men and women
to know the truth which sets them free. We come to get our
lives into balance again, for the pressures of the world spoil
our equilibrium. We, whose vision is often so easily and
effectively distorted, want to get our lives into focus again.
Help us now to see Jesus whom death could not defeat, whose
light pierces every darkness in the world, and whose love
conquers every hatred. Enable us, Father, to see him; and
seeing him, to see ourselves.

Help us now, therefore, to examine our hearts with honesty,
and to see more clearly the things that enslave us, for we
can be so repentant about trifling sins, so sorry for the
small, foolish sins, and yet so utterly blind to our real
sins — the cavalier way in which we overlook the injustices
from which others suffer, but from which we ourselves are
mercifully free; the casualness with which we use others for
our own ends; the classification of people as those who are
good to know and those who are not good to know; above all,
the failure to feel for all who are persecuted and tyrannized
over in so many countries in the world.

We do not deserve forgiveness, Lord, yet is your love so great,
so unutterably great, that your forgiveness is ours for the
asking. Lord, we ask forgiveness, in your name.

13

God of mercy; make us men and women of integrity, so that, discerning the true from the false, we may hold on to the truth. Release us into the freedom of God's children that we may honour Christ before all men's eyes.

And let his mind and his spirit be in us always.

AMEN

Prayer (2)

In our present world, there are multitudes who crave for a freedom which is not theirs. Freedom from fear, from persecution, from themselves.

Let us remember all such in our prayers.

Lord Jesus Christ help us to hear again your promise that you came to bring liberty to the captives and to open the doors of prisons to them that are bound.

We think of all who are unjustly condemned and imprisoned in such places as South Africa, Greece, and Russia; men and women whose only crime is their belief in the right of men to be free.

We think of such organizations as Amnesty International with groups of men and women all over the world, working for the release of the innocent and the persecuted, and sending them messages of hope and encouragement.

As we think, we pray for all these, our brothers and sisters in distress.

We think of all who, because of these injustices rankling in their minds, have chosen violent means to redress wrongs, that they may learn a much better way. The way of love. For love conquers all. Love wins battles when no other way is possible. Let the Christ way of love come in to heal the world and to wean it from violence.

We think, too, of the cruel and dishonest who are in prison for crimes against others. We hope and pray that our prisons may become not so much places of punishment as of rehabilitation and reconciliation. And stir us all to a Christian concern for those who have done evil things.

14

We think of those who are captive to vicious habits, not because they are evil, but because they are weak. Keep us from self-congratulation that we are not as they are, and from feeling superior and good because we are different. But show us how we can help them, our brothers and sisters, to be free again.

We think of those who are captive to money, to power, to lust, to selfish ambition, to evil moods, to anxieties and fears. The world is sick and needs healing. We believe, Lord, you can give this healing. Heal us, therefore, from everything that destroys life in us. And make us whole.

We think of all imprisoned by sorrow and care. Release them and bring them the joy and freedom that comes from knowing you as their friend and Saviour.

We ask this in the name of Jesus, the Lord and giver of life.

AMEN

Prayer before Sermon
We listen to your Word, Lord, not to confirm us in our own prejudices or to save us from pain, but to know the truth without which we are never free.

Offertory Prayer
We claim, Lord, to love you. Let that claim be evident in our lives by keeping free from the claims that things make upon us. And grant that this money, freely given, may save the lives of some, and so perform its healing ministry.

Benediction
    May God the Father bless you:
    May Christ the Son take care of you:
    The Holy Spirit enlighten you all the days of your life.
    The Lord be your defender and keeper of body and soul
    both now and for ever
    and to the ages of ages. AMEN

5

First Prayer

'He is faithful that called you.
The Lord is faithful: he will strengthen you and guard you
from evil.
He is faithful who promised.'

O God our Father, we worship you in wonder and in love.
Our minds cannot contain you, nor our words express you.
Yet in Christ we see your glory, and hear your Word,
and know your love.
Open our eyes to see you now;
Open our ears to hear your command;
Open our hearts to love you more,
through Jesus Christ our Lord.

We come to you, O God, burdened by the memory of things
we have done or failed to do.
We have been thoughtless of the needs of others;
we have been impatient of the faults of others;
we have been despondent and easily cast down.
We have not worked as we ought;
we have not loved as we ought;
we have not prayed as we ought;
we have not lived as we pray.
Forgive us, O God, as now we lay on you the burden of our sins
Help us to hate them; then give us the assurance that they
are forgiven, through Jesus Christ our Lord.

O Lord our God, we seek your guidance and your strength
for all that the days shall bring:
Give us a quiet mind amid the noise and tumult
of our daily lives.
Give us strength of spirit that we may strive
for what we know to be right.
Give us the gift of sympathy for all who are in need,
especially for those among whom we dwell.

Give us such faith in you
that amid all uncertainty of mind and fear of heart
we may yet trust in you as children in a Father well beloved.

Grant these our prayers, O God,
and with them the unspoken prayers of every heart,
through Jesus Christ our Lord.
OUR FATHER . . . . . .

Second Prayer
For all your goodness and your grace we thank you, O God.
For life and health, for home and friends;
For all the good provision of your providence by which
we are sustained from day to day;
For every pure and lovely joy with which
you have enriched our lives, especially any such that now
make glad our hearts when we remember them.
For all these earthly blessings, God, we thank you.

But, more than all of these, for this we give you praise:
That through Christ Jesus you have come to us in human form,
thus to reveal your love;
That in his life and death and triumph over death
you have declared your purpose for us all,
to mould us to his likeness so that we may share his life.
For this, our holy calling and high destiny
we thank you in humility and awe,
through Jesus Christ our Lord.

Father, now we bring to you in prayer the needs
of all your children everywhere.

We pray for all the millions, strangers to us but known
and loved by you, who this day starve while we and others
waste our bread. Let not our conscience rest at peace
until the bountiful harvest of the earth is freely shared
with every child of need.
We pray for all who suffer through the violence of men.

Root out from all men's hearts the bitterness and prejudice,
the envy and hatred that make for war.
Cleanse our land from injustice and impurity,
and give peace in our time, O Lord.

We pray, O God, for your Church throughout the world.
Where it is strong, make it gentle:
    where it is weak, make it strong.
Where it is honoured, make it humble:
    where it is persecuted, make it proud.
Where it is wrong, over-rule it:
    where it is right, make it stand.

O God we bring to you the needs
of those whose lives are shadowed by sorrow,
remembering especially any known to us who need our prayers:
    those whose sickness finds no cure;
    those whose sadness finds no comfort;
    those whose loneliness cannot be filled;
    those who in bitterness will not forget;
Bind up their wounds, Lord, and lift their hearts to you,
as now in silence we remember them.

Eternal God, whom we trust, not for this world alone;
we thank you for all those dear to us
who through the mystery of death have passed to you.
Let us not forget them, Lord, nor think them far away.
Make real to us the fellowship we share with them
in fellowship with you, and, when this life is done,
bring us to life with them in you,
through Jesus Christ our Lord.

Glory to the Father, and to the Son, and to the Holy Spirit,
as it was in the beginning, is now, and ever shall be,
world without end.　　AMEN

6

Prayer of Approach, Confession and Supplication
He that doeth the will of God abideth for ever.
This is life eternal that we may know God
and Jesus Christ whom he has sent.
Blessed be thou, O God, who hast made known through Jesus
Christ the mystery of thy will.
Blessed be thou, O God, who hast delivered all things into
his hands and hast declared thine eternal purpose to bring
all things to perfection in him.
Blessed be thou, O God, in whose will is our peace.

In thy presence, O God, we confess our sins and the sins of
our world.
O merciful Father who in Christ didst look upon the weaknesses of men more in pity than in anger and more in love
than in pity; look thus upon us, for in our folly we have
ignored thy holy will and gone our own way and found no
peace. We have been anxious about many things and neglected
those things which truly belong to our health and salvation.
In a technical age we have despised the techniques of Christ
and vastly underrated thy most excellent gift of love, the
very bond of peace and of all virtues.
            Lord have mercy upon us.

Almighty and everlasting God, whose throne is eternity, and
the farthest heavens thy dwelling-place, yet who abidest in
every faithful and humble heart: open our eyes, we pray
thee, that we thy children may know the things eternal to be our
inheritance, and the lowliest place, where thou art, to be
our Father's house; to whom be dominion and glory, world
without end.
O Christ, the everlasting Son of the Father, our King: enthrone
thy presence in our hearts, that the hatred of sin, the love
of thy will, the light of truth and the joy of the Holy Ghost
may be ours as thine, and thou rule in thine own Kingdom
for ever and ever.   AMEN

Prayer of Thanksgiving, Intercession and Thanksgiving for the Departed

I will magnify thee, O God, my King and I will praise thy name for ever and ever.

Every day will I give thanks to thee, and praise thy name for ever and ever.

Great is the Lord, and marvellous worthy to be praised: there is no end of his greatness . . . . . .

The Lord is gracious and merciful, long-suffering and of great goodness.

The Lord is loving unto every man, and his mercy is over all his works.

The Lord is nigh unto all them that call upon him; yea all such as call upon him faithfully.

He will fulfil the desire of them that fear him: He also will hear their cry and will help them.

Let all flesh give thanks unto his holy name for ever and ever.

Let us pray God, through Jesus Christ our Lord, that having laid the strong foundations of the Church he would protect her always, that she may neither be undermined by error, nor shaken by any storm of the world.

> Lord in thy mercy
> *Hear our prayer.*

Let us pray God, through Jesus Christ our Lord, (that he would bless the Queen and all her house,) that he would put a spirit of wisdom and understanding into the hearts of our leaders, that he would make us bold in the pursuit of prosperity but sensitive to the needs of unemployed men, that he would give to our people a vision and carve out for us again a place in the world.

> Lord in thy mercy
> *Hear our prayer.*

Let us pray God, through Jesus Christ our Lord, that he would bring peace to the world and hope for the future.

20

Lord in thy mercy
Hear our prayer.

Let us pray God, through Jesus Christ our Lord, that he would keep company with the companionless and the anxious and the sick and the mourners and the refugees, and with all whom we love.

Lord in thy mercy
Hear our prayer.

Eternal God, with whom are the issues of life; we give thee thanks for all thy saints who, having in this life witnessed a good confession, have left the light of their example to shine before thy people; especially those beloved by us who are now with thee. Bring us into communion with them here in thy presence; and enable us so to follow them in all godly living, that hereafter we may with them behold thy face in glory and in the heavenly places be one with them for ever: through Jesus Christ our Lord in whose words we are bold to pray and to say
OUR FATHER . . . . . .

7

First Prayer
Eternal God, thou maker of men, and re-maker of men, we worship thee. Before thee all masks fall, all vanities are stripped away, all pretences are utterly exposed. Thou art light. We turn towards thy light as men who have been long in the dark, and ask for forgiveness, clarity and insight — the gifts of light — to fall upon us in our worship.

O Lord, what can be done about people like us? What can be done about those who have deliberately turned their backs on things that belong to their peace? What can be done about those who once gaily volunteered 'Yes, I'll go', but who, when the need arose have simply not gone? What can be done about those who have said 'Lord, Lord' so often in worship,

but who have then hacked our neighbour down with our tongue
and crucified him with our coldness of heart? What can be
done when we are aware of these things, but are paralysed in
will and cannot change ourselves?

We give thanks today, remembering that what can be done, **has**
been done in Christ, and **is** done for ever. We claim
across all our emptinesses the power of the resurrection. We
pray, over all our sins, for the mercy of the Cross. We ask,
in thy name, for a new beginning, and a new day, and a new
heart.

OUR FATHER . . . . . .

Second Prayer
O God, our help in ages past, our hope for years to come,
help us now to lean upon the rod and staff of thine eternal
compassion as we say our prayers.

We give thanks for everything today that lifts the heart
and makes life worth living. For thy beauty in the loveliness
of the world; for thy wisdom breaking through the discoveries
of men; for thy love made clear again at Easter in the figure
of Jesus Christ, broken and crucified, risen and triumphant,
we say now that we are unspeakably grateful to thee.

For all happiness in which we are allowed to share; for home
and friends, for the joy of loving and being loved, we give
thee thanks. For signs of thy presence dropped broadcast
through the world in the most unexpected places; for all insights, sacramental and oblique, that have broken open and
gleamed from the printed page; for the mystery of music and
the sudden strange power of art; for the bush that burns at
our feet and is never consumed — we speak our unspeakable
thanks to thee.

We pray for those whose faith is sorely tried; whose hopes
have suffered wreck; whose love is strained to breaking.
We pray for those who cry for comfort because their heart's
desire has been withheld or taken away. Grant them that faith
which never fails; that hope which no change or loss can

touch; that love which beareth all things; and bring them
through all rain and darkness by the clear light of thy
mercy and protection, through Jesus Christ our Lord.

We commit to thee in our prayers all young people everywhere,
and those who lead them. May they grow in wisdom as in stature,
in strength of character and the knowledge and fear of the Lord;
and so faithfully quit themselves like men and serve their
day and generation.

We pray for our nation and all nations. May a new era dawn,
and a new and more excellent way open out before the peoples
of the earth. O Lord of the nations, stoop and move amongst
us in mercy and renewal, that hope may come like a rising
dawn across our darkened earth.

We commit our loved ones into thy keeping, wherever they
may be. Allow us, in our human loves and affections, to be
able to perceive more and more the quality of the love of
God.
Glory be to the Father . . . . . .

8

Let us worship God. God has shined into our hearts to give
the light of the knowledge of the glory of God in the face
of Jesus Christ.

Adoration, Confession, Absolution, Petition
Lord God, we come to adore you.
You hold us in being and without you we could not be. Before
time and the universe began, you were. When time is finished
and the universe is no more, you will still be. Nothing can
rob you of your power. We are silent before the immensity
and mystery of your being . . . . . .

All-loving and most generous Father, rather than your excellent
way we have taken our own proud, headstrong way; and when,
as now, we stop to think, we know we are in danger of damna-
tion. We have cared and go on caring far more for our own
wishes than for your will. There isn't a thing in our possession, either material or spiritual, that isn't your gift,
but we have behaved as those who reckon all this our own to
do with as we like and we have not hesitated to insult you
with our left-overs and our small change. We seldom dare to
expect what you have promised or to attempt what you have plain
bidden. And we have been very well pleased with ourselves.

> Lord, have mercy upon us.
> Christ, have mercy upon us.
> Lord, have mercy upon us.

To all who are thoroughly disgusted with their self-centredness
and, knowing that this is their only hope of liberation from
it, pledge themselves anew to Jesus Christ, the forgiveness
of sins is proclaimed, in the name of the Father and of the
Son and of the Holy Ghost.
Lord come to us to cleanse us. Come to us to heal us.
Come to us to strengthen us. Come to us to employ us.
And grant that having received you we may not again run away
from you into conceit or callousness, folly, snobbery,
childishness or pride but be your loyal men and women tomorrow
and the next day and for ever: (*Ascription follows*)

Intercessions:
Hear, O God, we pray, the intercessions we make in the name
of Christ and so that his kingdom may come amongst men.
We pray for your holy Church. Give her grace to bear to
the peoples of the world, even in the earthen vessels of her
members' lives, the joyful wine of real faith in you and of
the gladness that can only be found in serving you.

We pray for your servant Elizabeth and all the royal family;
for the Prime Minister, the government and parliament; the
Lord Provost and Magistrates of our city, the Lord Lieutenant

and Convener of our county; and all others anywhere in
authority in the world. Give them the insight and courage so
as to glorify you in the way they go about their duty.

We pray for the friendless, the homeless and the weary; the
aimless, the spiritless and the sad; the childless, the hopeless
and the mentally sick; that still, as of old, you will prove
yourself to them Saviour alike of the body as of the soul.

We pray for all who stand on the threshold of opportunities:
brides and bridegrooms; fathers and mothers; those who have
found new work, new friends, new faith: fulfil in them your
promise of life in overflowing abundance. We remember especially
any such as are known to ourselves whom, with all who are near
and dear to us, we name in the silence of our hearts . . . . . .
Be with them, we pray, and help them; through Jesus Christ
our Lord, to whom with the Father and the Holy Ghost be all
glory, dominion and power, world without end.

Thanksgiving, Consecration, Oblation, Commemoration

> The Lord be with you
> *And also with you.*
> Lift up your hearts
> *We lift them up unto the Lord.*
> Let us give thanks unto the Lord God
> *It is meet and right so to do.*

We thank you, God, that you can never be untrue to yourself
and that this is why you have always loved and cannot but
always go on loving the world you have made. We thank you that
in Jesus all of this love that can be contained in a human
life was fully and most gloriously expressed. We thank you
that he was known as the friend of those whom most men despised, and that he shared his plans and his work with ordinary
men and women like ourselves. Praying that we may never let
him down, we thank you for the honour of being called his
friends. And we would join our voices with the great company
of heaven always praising and singing to you:

> *Holy, holy, holy, Lord God of hosts:*
> *Heaven and earth are full of your glory:*
> *Glory be to you, O Lord most high.*

Wherefore, O God, we ask you to accept this offering of worship
that we make in your name and to send down your Holy Spirit,
the Lord and giver of life, to bless and consecrate our bodies,
minds and spirits that we may give ourselves to you a living
sacrifice, holy and without blemish, which is our reasonable serv

Preserve, O God, the catholic Church in unity and peace, in
holiness and truth, free from persecution or glorious under it;
that she may advance the honour of the Lord Jesus, for
ever represent his sacrifice and glorify his person and, filled
with his spirit, share in his victory.

We remember all our dear ones whom we have loved and lost.
Grant that they and we may, at last, together come to those
good things that pass man's understanding but which you have
prepared for those who love you; through Jesus Christ our
Lord, in whose words we make bold to pray together saying:
OUR FATHER . . . . . .

9

This is the day that the Lord has made. Let us rejoice and
be glad in it!

Let us pray:
O God our Father how wonderful you are! We recollect with jo
that this first day of the week you looked upon all your
creation and saw it was good. We rejoice too in the light that
awakens us every new day, and that more precious light that
shines in Jesus Christ.

O God our Father how wonderful you are! We recollect with jo
that on this day you raised Jesus from the dead. Raise us, we
ask you, into a new dimension of living, a new vitality of
faith.

O God our Father how wonderful you are! We recollect with joy
that on this first day of the week you gave your spirit to men.
Fill us now with that same spirit that we may be renewed.

Dear Father, forgive us for neglecting the things of the spirit
this past week. Having praised you with our lips we failed to
praise you with our hands and minds. We failed to bring glory
to you by the quality of our work or our concern for others.
Forgive us Father.

We change from mood to mood, and sometimes we begin to realize
how thin is the veneer of holiness, how thick the depth of
worldliness in our lives.

Lord it's natural to be selfish — make us to know we are sons
of God made for higher ways than instinct and mood demand,
and forgive our sin.

Lord it's natural to forget our promises — make us to remember
your great love that will never forget us or let us go,
and forgive our sin.

Lord it's natural to be two-faced and to serve you when it
suits us — tell us Lord that nothing can ever separate us from
the single-minded devotion of him who was torn asunder for
our sake upon a cross. So bring us closer to the mind and
spirit of the Master this coming week,
through Jesus Christ our Lord.   AMEN

Prayer of thanks and intercession
O God our Father you surround us each day with so many lovely
things, we offer you our praise and thanks for the glory of
the seasons, their regularity, their wonderful variation: the
warmth of summer sun, the colours of autumn, the sparkle of
winter snow and ice, the freshness and renewed vitality of the
spring. All nature breathes its praise of our Creator, and so
we rejoice to join our thanks with that of hill and sea, bird
and animal.

We rejoice, Father, in the loveliness of man-made things: the
hum of a dynamo running smooth, the breathless wonder of moon

rocket, the beauty of a painting, a song, a piece of furniture, the marvel of medicines and the renewal of sick bodies by surgeon's skill, the intricacy of needlework, the power of oratory, the love of mother for her child, the compassion of men for the needy — for all that makes the world around us fascinating and radiant with hope for the future, for all that reflects the heart and mind of a loving creator, a caring Father.

Bless every endeavour of man's to make this world a better place to live in. Bless his creative work so that good may banish the destructive elements in our society. Especially bless those who bring beauty and warmth to those places where there is coldness and ugliness. We remember the work of social workers, housing conveners, police, district nurses, probation officers, youth leaders, and those who give their time to help the aged, infirm, house-bound.

Lord it's a lovely world for most of us. We remember today those whose world is dark and sombre. Bless all old people in this area who have few friends, fewer as the years progress and as their friends part this life one by one. Be with all newcomers who find it hard to make friends, and so let each of us here dedicate ourselves to offering the word and hand of friendship to all who live near us — remembering that we too were once in need of friends, through Jesus Christ our Lord.

O Lord you have a word for those in the shadows. But you have a word for those who are successful and in good spirits. Speak this day to those upon whom the sun is shining, that they be kept from pride and self-conceit. Speak to those so sure they are right and others are wrong that they be given the spirit of tolerance. May all whose lives are full of fun and meaning and promise know that they are not their own but are bought with a price, and so learn to share the fruits of their happiness. Tell them, tell us all that man's true happiness is founded on him who is the Way, the Truth and the Life, even on him who will purify and hallow success and bring opportunity and victory out of failure, even Jesus Christ our Lord.

And finally we offer our thanks for all the faithful who have
departed this life in the fear of the Lord, and our own
beloved who live and serve in your nearer presence. Keep us
and them in one unbroken fellowship of heart. Grant us always
to wait for you, to keep vigil for you, so that at your coming
we may be found ready, through Jesus Christ our Lord to whom
with the Father and the Holy Spirit be given the praise and
the glory. AMEN

10

A Prayer of Thanksgiving
Father, we thank you now for all that you have given us.
We thank you
for the changing beauty of the world,
the beauties of cloud and sunshine, night and day.

We thank you
for all the talents and powers you have given to men,
and for all the use to which these talents have been put.

We thank you
for showing us your love for us and for all men,
for teaching us to love each other,
and for all the love that we give and receive each day.

Most of all we thank you
for Jesus:
for his life of love,
for his teaching and example,
for his death on the cross,
for the new life which he has brought to light,
and for all that we enjoy because of his perfect love.

Father, Son and Holy Spirit, three persons in one eternity of
love, we thank you, and will thank you, for ever.

A Prayer of Confession
Father, when we remember your great love,
and when we remember the command of Jesus that we should love
each other,
we are ashamed of the poverty of our own love.
We confess that love has not ruled in our hearts,
nor been the guiding principle in our lives.
We have not loved you, our God;
we have not loved our fellow men and women;
we have allowed our own personal wants and desires to blind
us to the needs of others.
Forgive us, Father, as we admit our failure and our sin,
our pride and our selfishness.
Forgive us in love that we may walk in love, for Jesus' sake.

A Prayer of Supplication
> Forgiveness does not mean
> Escape from consequences, but grace to face the
> consequences.'*

We believe, Father, that we have been forgiven:
in the strength of that forgiveness,
may we more clearly see the truth,
> more bravely face the world,
> more lovingly serve our neighbour,
> more joyfully follow Jesus.
In his name we ask it.   AMEN

A General Intercession
Father of us all,
we pray now for every man, woman and child in this world that
you have made.
We pray that as we speak of them we may remember that each
is himself,
known to you by name, loved and cared for by you,
Father of us all.
We pray
for Christian people everywhere, worshipping you in different
ways,

* From *The Old Man of the Mountains* by Norman Nicholson.

30

and too often separated from each other by man-made barriers.
We pray that we and all other Christians may trust in your
love,
and find strength to serve you and our fellowmen.

We pray
for all the people with whom we are associated in any way:
for parents and children, brothers and sisters, neighbours
and friends;
for our fellow-citizens in this city;
for our fellow-Scotsmen, and all the people of the United
Kingdom.
We remember especially those who govern us,
and who hold positions of responsibility and command among us.
We pray that we may be a nation and a people
inspired by the gospel of your love
with a vision of unity and brotherhood,
and that justice and compassion may rule our common life.

We pray for our fellowmen in other nations and with other
needs:
people like ourselves, in wealthy nations;
people living in daily hunger, in poorer nations.
We pray
that peace may prevail among the nations,
and that all men may accept each other as brothers,
so that the gospel of your love may inspire us all to a vision
of world-wide unity and brotherhood,
and that justice and compassion
may rule the common life of all the world.

We pray for people in special need.
Each need is different,
and we cannot remember them all:
we know that there are
          people who are ill, people who mourn,
          people who are lonely, people who are hungry or
          homeless,
          people who are afraid, people who are puzzled and
          anxious;

31

above all, we know that there are people
who cannot believe that they matter,
or that anyone cares about them.
We pray for them:
we want them all to know your love,
and we ask you to use us
to bring the assurance of your love
to all in need, whatever their need.

Father of us all, we have brought our prayers.
We cannot have remembered all who need our prayers;
and there is one thing we must ask before we end:
we want your will to be done,
and your love to be known,
wherever people live and love and work and laugh,
wherever people suffer and die.
May your will be done,
here and everywhere,
now and always.   AMEN

11

A Brief Prayer of Confession
Father, every day brings new evidence of your love:
to the eyes of faith, the whole of creation shows your
greatness;
to the ears of faith, the life of the world speaks of your
love;
to the mind of faith, history tells of your purpose.
Your Holy Spirit, at work in our world, is always active,
never silent.
Yet, Father, we have looked and looked, and seen nothing;
        we have heard and heard, and understood nothing;
foolishly we have been blind and deaf,

and have ignored your truth,
>your promises,
>your love.
Forgive us, Father, for the sake of Jesus our Lord.

A Brief Thanksgiving

We thank you, Father, for all our joy and all our longing.
You have given us in this world beauty and love;
you have also given us the ordinary, necessary things for
daily life.
We thank you, Father, not only for these things,
but for the gift of hope,
and for all that reminds us of your promise of eternal life;
through Jesus Christ our Lord.

A Brief General Intercession

Let us remember the needs of men and women and children everywhere:
the needs of the great and the powerful,
and the needs of the poor and the humble;
the needs of those who laugh,
and the needs of those who weep;
the needs of those who are rich,
and the needs of those who have nothing;
the needs of those who enjoy good health,
and the needs of those who suffer from pain and disease.
(*A brief silence*)
Father, we commend all these to your love,
praying that your will may be done;
and we pray that the Church,
the fellowship of Christian people, may be faithful,
and may find strength to do your will,
for Jesus' sake.   AMEN

SECTION B

Sacraments and Ordinances

1

SACRAMENT OF BAPTISM—FIRST ORDER

During the singing of a suitable hymn, the child is brought into the church, and the minister, standing at the font, says:

Dear people, hear the words of our Lord Jesus Christ who, after his resurrection and before his ascension, commanded his disciples saying:

> 'Full authority in heaven and on earth has been committed to me. Go forth therefore and make all nations my disciples; baptize men everywhere in the name of the Father and the Son and the Holy Spirit, and teach them to observe all that I have commanded you. And be assured, I am with you always, to the end of time.' (*Matt. 28:18-20. N.E.B.*)

Our Lord Jesus Christ, taking upon him the sins of the world, was baptized by John in the river Jordan, and anointed by the Holy Spirit for his saving work which he accomplished by his cross and resurrection.

Baptism is the sign of burial in the cleansing grace of Christ and of resurrection to a new way of life filled with the Holy Spirit.

Through baptism we become members of the Church which is body of Christ and are claimed for the Lord.

The blessing of Christ may be given to children. Consider what is written in the Gospels:

'They brought children for him to touch; and the disciples rebuked them first. But when Jesus saw this he was indignant and said to them, "Let the children come to me; do not try to stop them; for the kingdom of God belongs to such as these

I tell you, whoever does not accept the kingdom of God like a child will never enter it." And he put his arms round them, laid his hands upon them, and blessed them.'

It is the duty of those who present their children for baptism to confess the faith into which they are to be baptized, and to promise to bring them up in that faith, and in the way of Christ and his Church.

Then, the parents or other sponsors standing, the minister says to them:
Do you present this child to be baptized, earnestly desiring that he may be grafted into Christ as a member of his body the Church?
    Answer: I do.

Do you believe in one God, Father, Son, and Holy Spirit; and do you confess Jesus Christ as your Saviour and Lord?
    Answer: I do.

Do you promise, with the help of God, to teach this child the truths and duties of the Christian faith; and by prayer and example to bring him up in the life and worship of the Church?
    Answer: I do.

Then the minister says:
The Lord bless you and your child and enable you faithfully to keep these promises.

Then, addressing the congregation, he says:
Baptism lays solemn obligations upon you the People of God. Be faithful to your calling as members of the Church of Christ, so that this child, and all other children among you, may grow up in the knowledge and love of Christ. In acceptance of this responsibility, let all stand.

The minister then says:
Let us confess the faith.
The congregation recite the Apostles' Creed.

Then the minister calls the people to prayer saying:
>   Lift up your hearts.
>   *We lift them up to the Lord.*

It is right and good, Lord, that always we should give you
thanks, for your Son Jesus Christ took our nature, died and
rose again for our salvation, and gave us this sacrament
through which we are united with him in his body the Church,
and summoned in him to die to sin and to live to righteousness.
Through your Holy Spirit bless us and this water, and grant
that this child may be born again of water and of the Holy
Spirit, and may always be found among your people; through
Christ our Lord.

Lord Jesus, the good shepherd, take this child into your flock,
and tend him always: Glory be to you, with the Father and
the Spirit, one God, evermore.   AMEN

*Then the parent, or other sponsor, presenting the child at
the font (the congregation standing) gives the
child's name to the minister. The minister, who may then take
the child into his arms, calls him by his Christian name or
names and pours or sprinkles water on his head, saying:*

N . . . . . . I baptize you in the name of the Father and the
Son and the Holy Spirit.   AMEN

The blessing of God Almighty, Father, Son and Holy Spirit, be
upon you always.   AMEN

*The congregation sing the Aaronic blessing. (Hymn 727
R.C.H.)*

*Then the minister, using the Christian name or names and the
surname of the child baptized, says:*

According to Christ's commandment N . . . . . . M . . . . . . is no
received into membership of the holy catholic Church, and
is engaged to confess the faith of Christ crucified, and to
be his faithful soldier and servant to his life's end.

Let us pray.

God most good, whose promises are not only to us, but also to
our children: we give you thanks that this child has been
received into the Church and sealed as your own. We rejoice
that he is grafted into Christ. Let the Holy Spirit strengthen

him, that he may grow into Christ and yield faith and love to his glory. Guide him through the years, and bring him in due time to the holy table to receive the communion of the body and blood of the Lord Jesus and to confess him boldly before men.

Father, whose own true Son was reared in a home at Nazareth: we pray for the home of this child, and for his parents. May his home always be filled with love, joy, and peace. May his parents always be mindful of his every need. May they by their teaching and example bring him up in Christian knowledge and obedience.

Merciful God, in whose Church there is one Lord, one faith, and one baptism: grant us always to acknowledge the lordship of your Son Jesus Christ, to confess with our whole lives the one true faith, and to live in love and unity with all who have been baptized in his name; through the same Jesus Christ, to whom, with you, Father, and the Spirit, be glory, evermore.   AMEN.

A hymn or doxology is sung
The Benediction

2
SACRAMENT OF BAPTISM— SECOND ORDER

(In the context of the worship of a congregation where both adults and children may be present)
Call to Worship
Opening Praise (a song or hymn suitable for children)
Opening Prayer
Praise (a baptismal song or hymn, during which those to be baptized are brought into church)

Opening Statement: (the people sitting)
Our authority for this sacrament of baptism is given in the
words of Jesus to his disciples, after his resurrection,
when he said:

> 'All power in heaven and on earth has been given
> to me. You, then, are to go and make disciples of
> all the nations and baptize them in the name of the
> Father and of the Son and of the Holy Spirit. Teach
> them to observe all that I have commanded you, and
> remember, I am with you always, even to the end of
> the world.' (*Matt. 28: 18-20. Phillips*)

What Jesus told his disciples to do then, we seek faithfully
and joyfully to do today. And in baptism, God declares that w
are all his children through Christ; that our future lies with
him through the Holy Spirit; and that the Church is the place
where we will be equipped to serve him in the world.

Little children do not understand these things now; but God's
promises do not depend on age and understanding; and in fact
he comes to them through his Word, and through his Spirit
working in the lives of their parents, and all who know and
love them, both within the Church and outside it.

But it is the parents whom he calls most clearly to help him
in his work. Will the parents therefore please stand, and take
their promises?

The Promises: (the parents standing)
Do you confess your faith in God, as your Creator and Father
in Jesus as your Saviour and Lord;
and in the Holy Spirit as your guide and helper?

Do you promise, with God's help, to bring this child up
as a Christian;
to teach him by word and example what this means;
and to help to bring him into full membership of God's Chur

As a congregation, we are also involved in the Christian upbringing of this child. We are called to help his parents in

their God-given task; to be the sort of Christian congregation
which he will be proud to join; and to set a good and joyful
example to him of Christian brotherhood, love and service.

Will you signify your renewed commitment to this calling, by
rising and standing in your places?'

*Act of baptism: (the congregation standing, and the
father holding the child and presenting him to the minister)*
N . . ., I baptize you in the name of the Father, and of the
Son, and of the Holy Spirit.
(the congregation reply) AMEN
*Blessing and declaration: (the minister now holding the
child, on behalf of the whole Church)*

According to Christ's commandment, N . . . is now received into
the membership of the holy catholic Church, and is committed
to following the way of the risen Christ unto his life's end.

(The congregation then say or sing the blessing)
*Prayer (a short prayer of thanks, of committal, and
of renewal)*

*Praise (during which the newly baptized infants, and
the younger children in the congregation, may leave: the parents
stay for the rest of the service)*

Scripture

Sermon

The Offering

Prayer of Intercession

Praise

Benediction

39

3

SACRAMENT OF BAPTISM—THIRD ORDER

'By baptism we were buried with Christ, . . . in order
that as he was raised from the dead . . . so also we might set
our feet upon the new path of life' (*Rom. 6:4 N.E.B.*)

We do this in response to the command of the risen Jesus:
'Full authority in heaven and on earth has been committed to
me. Go forth therefore and make all nations my disciples;
baptize men everywhere in the name of the Father and the Son
and the Holy Spirit, and teach them to observe all that I have
commanded you. And be assured, I am with you always, to the
end of time.' (*Matt. 28:18-20: N.E.B.*)

In baptism we are remembering how Jesus came through death
and shares his victory with us.

In baptism we are celebrating the coming of this child into
the life of his family, into the life of the Church, into the
new path of life upon which the Spirit of God now leads us.

Prayer
Almighty God, Creator, Saviour, Spirit: bless us, and what we
now do, and the means we use; and by the water of baptism
make this child one with yourself and one with us; through
Jesus Christ our Lord.

Promises
For parents:
Do you believe in one God, Father, Son and Holy Spirit; and
do you confess Jesus Christ as your Lord and Saviour?

Do you promise, relying on the grace of God, to teach your
child the truths and duties of the Christian faith; and by
your prayers and your example to bring him up in the life and
worship of the Church?

For the congregation:
This sacrament lays solemn obligations on you, the people of
God. Will you do your part, so that this child may grow up to
know and trust Christ? To show you accept this responsibility,
will you stand?

Baptism
This is A B . . .
A B, I baptize you in the name of the Father and the Son and
the Holy Spirit . . .

The blessing of God Almighty descend upon you and dwell in
your heart for ever.

We have done as Christ commanded, and this child is now
received into the membership of his Church, and commended to
your care as a congregation of the Church.

'The Lord bless you and keep you . . .' *(sung by congregation)*

Prayer
Gracious God, we give thanks for this child in whom you have
shown us again the meaning of our faith and the signs of new
life. Lead him forward now to live the life that awaits him,
secure and free in the power of the risen Jesus.

Guide and keep the family to whom you have given him, and
give to them all a sense of your love and grace with them.

Touch us all with the promise of this sacrament – that the
old ways in us have lost their power, and that in Christ we
are being made to rise above our failures and set our feet upon
the new path of life.

Therefore as he taught us we pray together, and say:
OUR FATHER . . . . . .

4

ADMISSION TO FIRST COMMUNION

(This will take place during a service of Public Worship, usually towards the close. The Kirk Session is constituted before the service, as this is an act of the Kirk Session.)

The minister says to the Congregation:
We are now going to admit to the privilege of sharing in the Lord's Supper, and to all the responsibilities of their commitment to Christ, the following:

(The names are read. As his name is read, each one rises and comes forward to stand in front of the minister.)
They have all been taught the faith and ways of the Church, and are now ready to declare in public the faith in which they were once baptized. Let us then support them with our prayers, and as they make their promises, remember that these are our promises too.

Let us pray.
Father of Jesus Christ, Father of all, as it is by your goodness that our life finds purpose, and by your love that we are called into the service of love, let the spirit of Jesus take hold of all your children, that they may grow in true goodness and become strong in love, through Jesus Christ our Lord.   AMEN

The minister then says to the new communicants:
Today we are looking back to your baptism, because then already you were claimed for God, as his children and members of the Church of Jesus Christ; and now we rejoice to see the fruit of your Christian upbringing, and of your own testing of its truth, because, by God's goodness, you have come to the point when you are ready freely to confess your own faith, and to claim Jesus as your Lord.

So today we also look forward, to your sharing with this

congregation (and with the whole Church of God) in its worship, work and witness, to your place at the Lord's table, and to the offering of your lives in his service.

Jesus said 'If anyone declares himself for me in the presence of men, I will declare myself for him in the presence of my Father in heaven.' Will you then declare yourselves for him and before him, as you answer the questions I now put to you—

> Do you declare your faith in Jesus Christ as your Lord and Saviour, in his God and Father as your God and Father, and in his Spirit as the source of life and love?
>
> *Answer: I do. (The answer may be made separately, by each of the candidates in turn.)*

> Do you promise, in that faith and by that Spirit, to live in God's love, and to serve him in your daily life?
>
> *Answer: I do.*

> Will you be a faithful member of the Church of God, sharing in its worship and service, giving of yourself in every way; and will you seek the fellowship of the Church wherever you are?
>
> *Answer: I will.*

The minister asks the congregation to stand, and says to the new communicants:
You have declared your faith; now in the name of the Lord Jesus Christ, the King and Head of his Church, I declare you to be admitted to the privilege of sharing in the Lord's Supper.

Will you now kneel, while we ask God's blessing on each and every one of you?

(It is possible to ask a different blessing over each candidate, and to call each by name. Texts from the New English Bible or another modern translation, can be used, suitably modified. Among those suitable are Rom. 15:13, Phil. 4:19; 1 Thess. 3:12-13, 5:13; 2 Thess. 2:17; 1 Pet. 5:10; 2 Pet. 1:2; Heb. 13:20-21.)

The Congregation sings the blessing:
The Lord bless you and keep you ...

The new communicants stand, and the minister says:
Our welcome to you is expressed in the right hand of fellowship.

(*The minister and Kirk Session (or representatives) shake hands with each new communicant, after which the communicants take their places with their families or friends in the congregation, being welcomed by then with a handshake, or in any appropriate way.*)

Let us pray.

Father of Jesus Christ, Father of all, we praise you for bringing these children of yours to this hour of dedication, and for giving us the joy of welcoming them. We are thankful for their baptism, for their homes, for every good influence on their lives, and for the joy and the love that they themselves have brought to others.

Now by your Spirit build us up together in faith and truth and love, that by our life and by our witness, others may come to rest and rejoice in Christ, and to share at his table and in his service, through Christ our Lord.   AMEN

5

CONFIRMATION SERVICE

(Compiled and adapted from *The Book of Common Order* 1940, *A Book of Services and Prayers* 1959, and *The Presbyterian Service Book* 1968.)

In the name of the Lord Jesus Christ and in accordance with the decision of the Kirk Session of this congregation we are about to admit to communicant membership of the Christian Church those persons gathered before me now. They have been under special instruction in the teaching of the Church and are now ready to profess publicly their faith in Jesus Christ.

The New Communicants will stand

In baptism you have already been received into the fellowship of Christ. You were then sealed as members of the family and household of God, and were engaged to be the Lord's. Now you come, of your own free will, to profess your faith in the Lord Jesus Christ, to consecrate yourselves to him, and to accept the privileges and responsibilities of membership of his Church.

I ask you therefore to make your profession of faith and to answer before God and this congregation the questions which now I put to you.

(The questions which follow should have the official sanction of the denomination of the church into which the New Communicant is to be received and should have been the subject of detailed study in the 'special instruction' already mentioned.)

1. Do you believe in one God, Father, Son and Holy Spirit; and do you confess Jesus Christ as your Saviour and Lord? *Answer*: I do.

2. Do you promise to join regularly with your fellow Christians in worship on the Lord's Day?

3. Do you promise to be faithful in reading the Bible, and in prayer?

4. Do you promise to give a fitting proportion of your time, talents and money for the Church's work in the world?

5. Do you promise, depending on the grace of God, to confess Christ before men, to serve him in your daily work, and to walk in his ways all the days of your life?

The Lord bless you and give you grace faithfully to perform these solemn promises.

Let us pray
O God, our Father, whose we are and whom we seek to serve, grant your blessing to those who now come to you in faith. Give them all joy and peace in believing; enlighten their minds that they may know you; nerve their wills that they

may serve you; kindle their hearts that they may love you, through Jesus Christ our Lord.　AMEN.

The congregation will stand.
If you desire to consecrate yourself to Christ, to serve his Church and to share his table you will come forward as your name is called.

(*The Session clerk reads the names of the new communicants who come forward individually and kneel. Over each these words are spoken.*)

The God of all grace who has called you to his eternal glory confirm you to the end.

Seeing you have professed your faith before God and this congregation, I now declare you to be admitted to the communicant membership of the Church of Jesus Christ: and in particular, into the fellowship of his congregation in this place, in token of which we offer you the right hand of fellowship . . .

Let us pray
Eternal God, our heavenly Father, you have given your Son to be the Saviour of mankind. We thank you that you have granted your servants to know your love in Christ Jesus and to acknowledge him as their Lord. Send down upon them the gift of the Holy Spirit; deepen their faith in the gospel; establish them in the fellowship of your Church; give them joy in your service; and keep them steadfast to the end.

We confess, O Lord our God, that we have not loved you as we ought. Forgive us, and grant us grace that we may all renew our vows, give ourselves again to your obedience, and in our lives bear witness to the faith we profess with our lips, through Jesus Christ our Lord.　AMEN.

6

HOLY COMMUNION—FIRST ORDER

Jesus said:
Blessed are the pure in heart for they shall see God.

> Eternal and ever-blessed God, so restrain every
> wandering thought and so banish every evil thought,
> that we this day being pure in heart may see you.

We remember how Jesus the Risen Lord was known to his friends
in the breaking of bread; and how their hearts were set ablaze
as they talked with him on the road.

> Lord Jesus, here in this church today, make yourself
> known to us in the breaking of bread, so that,
> having met you here, we may go from this place with
> hearts aflame with love of you.
> This we ask for your love's sake: AMEN.

Praise

Prayer

If we tell God of our sin, we can depend on him in his goodness to forgive us. Let us ask forgiveness now.

> O God, our Father, there has been no part of this
> life of ours that has been fit for you to see.

In our homes

We have been careless and inconsiderate;
We have been moody and irritable and difficult to live with;
We have treated those whom above all we ought to cherish with
a discourtesy we would never dare to show to strangers;

> For this forgive us, O God.

At our work

We have not been as diligent as we should have been;
We have been afraid to think, and to follow only truth;
We have not always borne each other's burdens and forgiven
each other's faults;
Sometimes we have tried to offer to you and to men that which
cost us nothing:

> For this forgive us, O God.

In the Church
We have found your service sometimes a burden and not a deligh
We have not always shown the love that brothers ought to show
We have been so immersed in the details that we have some-
times lost the vision of the eternities;
We have often been too satisfied with self and too critical
of others:
> For this forgive us, O God.

In life in the world
We have so often been careless in duty;
> slack in prayer;
> blind to the things which should have been our chief
> concern;
In us there has been so little of the love which is the magnet
to draw men to you:
> For this forgive us, O God.
Let us be silent and in the silence let us make our own confession to God.
O God, our Father, we know that we are sinners, but we also
know that we are forgiven sinners; help us here and now to
accept the forgiveness and the absolution which you are
offering to us.
And help us to prove our penitence and our gratitude by going
from this place to live with something of the beauty of holiness and something of the loveliness of our Master upon us,
so that men may know that we have been with Jesus.

Reading Lessons

Prayer
The Lord upholds all those who are falling and raises up those
who are bowed down. Let us ask him for his help.
> O God, bless us and help us today.
Those whose minds are perplexed, and who have more questio
than they have answers;
Those who have temptations the power of which makes them
afraid;
Those whose hearts are sore and whose eyes have known tears:
> Bless all such, O God.

Those for whom things are easy, that they may be kept from
pride;
Those for whom things are difficult, that they be kept from
discouragement and despair;
Those who are regretful for the past or afraid of the future:
    Bless all such, O God.
Bless any in anxiety of mind;
      in pain of body;
      in distress of heart.
Bless your Church in this country and throughout all the world;
and so cleanse, purify and strengthen it that it may be a fit
weapon for your purposes.
Bless our country, our Queen and our leaders, and in the days
when decisions are difficult, guide them in the way that is
right.
Bless those we love and those who are dear to us.

The Silence

From our deep darkness come we to your light;
From all our weakness to your peace and power;
And from our sinfulness to your great love;
Fulfil your promise and turn none of us away:
    through Jesus Christ our Lord.   AMEN.

Praise

The Communion Hymn

The grace of the Lord Jesus Christ be with you all

Let us hear how Paul tells how this sacrament began:
The tradition which I have passed on to you goes right back
to the Lord. That tradition tells that on the night on which
he was being delivered into the hands of his enemies, the Lord
Jesus took a loaf, and when he had thanked God for it, he
broke it and said:
    This means my body which is for you.
You must continue to do this to make you remember me.
In the same way at the end of the meal he took the cup too,
and said:
    This cup stands for the new relationship with God
    made possible at the cost of my death.

You must continue to do this as often as you drink
it to make you remember me.
For every time you eat this loaf and drink this cup you are
publicly proclaiming the Lord's death until he comes again.

The Declaration of Faith
I come to the Lord's Table in obedience to the invitation and
command of Jesus Christ who suffered and died for me.
To him I owe the assurance that my sins are forgiven.
Through him I know that God is my heavenly Father.
On him alone I depend for grace to overcome all
evil and to do the right.
Within this fellowship and with all his followers
I will strive to maintain his honour upon earth.

As Jesus on the night on which he was betrayed took a common
loaf and a common cup of wine and used them to be the signs
of truth eternal, I take this bread and this wine to be set
apart from their common use to this their sacred use this day.
O God, our Father, we know that you are always
trying to speak to us in the common things and in
the common experiences of life, and that in the midst
of time you are always giving us glimpses of eternity.
So let your Spirit be in us and be upon this bread
and wine today that through them we may enter into
our blessed Lord and he into us, that
they may tell us of his sacrifice;
they may comfort us with his grace;
they may confirm us in his strength;
they may confront us with his love;
they may fill us with his life.

As Jesus gave thanks so let us give thanks.

O God, our Father, we thank you for this sacrament.
For all who down the centuries at this table have found
the light that never fades;
the joy that no man takes from them;
the forgiveness of their sins;
the love which is your love;
the presence of their Lord;
We thank you.

For all the means of grace:
> For the Church to be our mother in the faith;
> For your book to tell us of your ways with men;
> For the open door of prayer which you have ever set
> before us:
>> We thank you.

> For the memory of the unseen cloud of witnesses who
> compass us about;
> And for the presence still with us of those who are
> an inspiration.
>> We thank you.

> That you have made us as we are;
> For the dream that will not die;
> That somehow we cannot sin in peace;
> That even in the mud we are haunted by the stars.
>> We thank you, O God.

For Jesus Christ our blessed Lord:
> That he who knew no sin was made sin for us,
> that he came to seek and to save that which was lost;
> that he gave his life a ransom for many;
> that he was obedient even to death, the death of the
> cross;
> that having loved his own he loved them to the end:
>> We thank you.

> That he lived;
> that he died;
> that he rose again;
> that he is with us to the end of time and beyond;
> and that he is with us here today:
>> We thank you.

Bless the Lord, O my soul, and never forget what he has done
for you; even so, Bless the Lord.
Hear this our thanksgiving through Jesus Christ our Lord.

AMEN

The Invitation

Come, not because you are strong, but because you are weak;
Come, not because any goodness of your own gives you a right
to come, but because you need mercy and help;
Come, because you love the Lord a little and would like to
love him more.
Come, because he loved you and gave himself for you.
Lift up your hearts and minds above your cares and fears and
let this bread and wine be to you the token and pledge of the
grace of the Lord Jesus Christ, the love of God and the
fellowship of the Spirit, all meant for you if you will receive
them in humble faith.

I will take the cup of salvation and call upon the Lord.
Blessed are they who hunger and thirst after righteousness
for they shall be filled.
O taste and see that God is good.

On the night on which he was being delivered into the hands
of his enemies Jesus took a loaf, and when he had thanked God
for it, he broke it and said: this means my body which is for
you. You must continue to do this to make you remember me.

     So eat all you of it and so remember.

In the same way at the end of the meal he took the cup and
said: this cup stands for the new relation with God made
possible at the cost of my death. You must continue to do
this as often as you drink it to make you remember me.

     So drink all you of it and so remember.

Every time you eat this loaf and drink this cup you are
publicly proclaiming the Lord's death until he comes again.

Let your light so shine before men that they may see your
lovely deeds and give the glory to your Father who is in
heaven.

Prayer

O God, our Father, send us from this place
    with the light of your hope in our eyes;
    and the fire of your love in our hearts.

Send us from this place
    conscious again of the unseen cloud of witnesses
    who compass us about;
    and certain of the presence of our blessed Lord.
Send us from this place
    sure of the forgiveness of sins
    and of the life eternal, to which there is no end.
Send us from this place
    sure that in this life you are with us
    and that afterwards you will receive us into glory.
OUR FATHER . . . . . .

7

HOLY COMMUNION—SECOND ORDER

(*A service such as in Section A should precede.*)

During the singing of a Psalm or Hymn the bread and wine
may be brought into the Church and laid on the table.
The minister shall unveil the elements and may say this prayer.

Let us pray
Almighty Father,
We are unworthy to celebrate this Sacrament,
But you have drawn near to us in Jesus Christ,
You have given him to us.
It is in his name that we draw near to you,
It is in obedience to his command,
That we offer this bread and this cup.
All that we have comes from you,
And what we give to you is your own.　　AMEN.

Then the minister shall say
    The grace of the Lord Jesus Christ be with you all.

    Dear Friends in Christ,

This is the record of the institution of this sacrament by
our Lord, as Saint Paul has handed it down to us:
For I received from the Lord what I also delivered to you,
that the Lord Jesus, on the night when he was betrayed, took
bread, and when he had given thanks, he broke it, and said
'This is my body which is for you. Do this in remembrance
of me.' In the same way also, the cup, after supper, saying
'This cup is the new covenant in my blood. Do this, as often
as you drink it, in remembrance of me.' For as often as you
eat this bread and drink the cup, you proclaim the Lord's
death until he comes. (R.S.V.)

> Let us then do as he has asked us:
> As he took bread and wine, I take this bread and
> this cup,
> And as he gave thanks and praise to God,
> Let us follow his example.

> > The Lord be with you
> > *And with you also.*
>
> > Lift up your hearts;
> > *We have lifted them up to the Lord.*
>
> > Let us give thanks to the Lord our God;
> > *It is right and fitting*

Father, all-powerful and ever-living God,
We do well always and everywhere to give you thanks
Through Jesus Christ our Lord.
With the great company of heaven,
With all your Church on earth,
And with the spirits of just men made perfect,
We worship and adore you, saying,
> 'Holy, Holy, Holy, Lord God of hosts,
> Heaven and earth are full of your glory,'
> Blessed be he who came, who comes, and who is yet to
We thank you that he was with you in the beginning,
That all things were made through him and for him,
And that in his image we were created men.
We thank you for all the blessings of life, known and unknown

For all who have loved us and enriched our lives,
Both the living, and the risen,
And above all, for your coming to us in Christ,
To live our life, to die our death,
And to rise again for us,
That our sins might be forgiven,
And that we might have eternal life,
Both now, and in your presence for ever.
We thank you that your Spirit is given to us,
That we may live as sons and daughters of the living God.

Having in remembrance all that Christ has done for us,
We rest in confidence on your eternal love
Declared to us once for all in him,
And we rely on his continual intercession for us.

And now, O Father, remembering these things,
We pray you to send you Spirit,
To bless both us and this bread and this wine,
that through them, in faith, we may receive the life of Christ.

Receive us, Father, as we offer to you our praise, our worship,
and our very selves,
For the sake of Christ who alone can make perfect our offering.

We pray to you as the Father of us all,
Remembering the whole world in its suffering and darkness,
And all in your vast kingdom who stand in need of your aid.

(*more intercessions here if desired or in prayer before
the sermon*)

Fulfil in all men the purpose of your redeeming love,
Renew in them the image and likeness of God,
Come speedily to save us,
So that all things in heaven and earth may be summed up in
Christ,
To whom with you and the Holy Spirit be glory for ever and
ever Amen.
And hear us as we pray together the Lord's Prayer,
OUR FATHER......

Then the minister shall say:
On the night when he was betrayed, our Lord Jesus instituted
this sacrament, and asked us to observe it, in remembrance
of him. Therefore we follow his example, who took bread,
> (*here the minister shall take the bread into his
> hands*),

blessed it, gave thanks, and broke it,
> (*here he shall break the bread*),

and said, 'This is my body which is for you. Do this in
remembrance of me.'

> (*here he shall raise the cup*),
In the same way also he took the cup, saying, 'This cup is
the New Covenant in my blood. Do this, as often as you drink
it, in remembrance of me.'

Lamb of God, you take away the sins of the world;
> *have mercy upon us.*

Lamb of God, you take away the sins of the world;
> *have mercy upon us,*

Lamb of God, you take away the sins of the world,
> *grant us your peace.*

(*Then the minister shall communicate himself in bread and
wine, and in giving them to the elders, or, at the moment
when he delivers them to the elders for the communion of the
people, he shall say:*),

The gifts of God for the people of God.

*When all have received, and the bread and wine have been
replaced on the table and covered, the Minister shall say:*

The peace of the Lord Jesus Christ be with you all.

Then he shall call the people to thanksgiving, saying:
Let us pray
Father, we thank you that once more you have fed us with
the bread of life.
We thank you for our fellowship with you, and with each other,
And with all the people of God, on earth and in heaven,
Especially those most dear to us,

Whom now for a little while we see no more.
We thank you that nothing can separate us from your love in
Christ,
And that the past, the present and the future are safe with
him
To whom with you and the Holy Spirit
Be glory and dominion throughout all ages,   AMEN.

Benediction. The minister shall say:
> Go in peace into the world, to love and serve the
> Lord.

8

HOLY COMMUNION—THIRD ORDER

*(At the top step of the vestry door, the two
elders preceding him, the minister shall pause and say, loudly:*)

Lift up your heads, ye gates; be lifted up, ye everlasting
doors: The King of Glory is coming in.

Who is this King of Glory?

(Then shall the minister reply:)
> The Lord of Hosts, he is the King of Glory.

*(Thereafter the minister receives the bread and wine; and
as the elders stand by the table he shall say:*)

From first to last this has been the work of God: he has reconciled us men to himself through Christ and he has enlisted us
in this service of reconciliation — we that were once far off
have been brought near through the shedding of Christ's
blood: for he is himself our peace. Therefore, that we may
be also reconciled in peace to one another, not in words
only but in action, we draw near to him and to one another.

The grace of the Lord Jesus Christ be with you all.

Behold, how good and joyful a thing it is, brethren, to live together in unity. We, who are many, are one bread, one body, for we all partake of the one bread.

The Lord Jesus, the same night in which he was betrayed, took bread: and when he had given thanks, he brake it and said, 'Take, eat; this is my body, which is broken for you: this do in remembrance of me.' After the same manner also he took the cup, when he had supped, saying, 'This cup is the new testament in my blood: this do ye, as oft as ye drink it, in remembrance of me.' For as often as ye eat this bread, and drink this cup, ye do shew the Lord's death till he come.

Therefore, that we may demonstrate that he has died for us, and that we may fulfil his blessed commandment and affirm our response to his invitation, in righteousness and joy we draw near to his table, in the name of the Father, and of the Son, and of the Holy Spirit.

As the Lord Jesus, the same night in which he was betrayed, took bread, I take these elements of bread and wine to be set apart from all common uses to this holy use and mystery: and as he lifted up his heart in praise and gladness, let us present to God our prayers and thanks.

Brethren, pray for me.

Let us pray
>Lift up your hearts;
>*We lift them up unto the Lord.*
>Let us give thanks unto our Lord God;
>*It is meet and right so to do.*

It is surely right. It is our true response that we now render to thee (Holy Lord, Father Almighty, Everlasting God), our adoration and our wonder. Therefore, in fellowship with believers in all ages and in all places, we praise thy glorious name, saying:

>Holy, holy, holy, Lord God of Hosts,
>Heaven and earth are full of thy glory,
>Glory be to thee, O Lord most high.

Blessed is he that cometh in the name of the Lord:
Hosanna in the highest.

Father in heaven, we declare thy works of mercy, and thy works
of love performed for us to win us from our ways of sin.
Here let us tell of Christ our Saviour, who came amongst us
to stand where we stand, to bless our children, and to share
our griefs; we bless thy name that he endured our sorrows and
was no stranger to our darkest night, that by his death upon
the Cross he redeemed us with his plenteous redemption, and
that by his rising again in glory he has shown us how to live
and how to die, and that by his giving us the Spirit of Truth,
the Comforter, he has given us the hope of his coming again.

Come to us, O Lord, in thy risen glory, and be our guest, the
guest of sinners: as we do now receive these gifts of bread
and wine, receive us into thy blessed kingdom, that we may
live from henceforth as thy redeemed, our past conquered and
our future kept in trust.

Send us thy Holy Spirit, whereby we may participate in this
event with meaning and with purpose; teach us that the bread
we eat speaks to us of community, that the bread which Jesus
broke he gave freely to a divided community, that they might
be one. And teach us, Father, that all who come to this bread
we break, though they may be strangers are brothers and friends
by its partaking.

Together we present to thee the sum and substance of our lives,
in private and in society, alone and in relationship, to be
accepted, used, and glorified by thee in service to our fellowmen and in the narrow way of Christ, whose yoke is easy, whom
to follow is to walk in light.

We fall alone: we fall together.
Together we shall be raised.

Lamb of God that takest away the sins of the world;
Have mercy upon us.
Lamb of God that takest away the sins of the world;
Have mercy upon us.
Lamb of God that takest away the sins of the world;
Grant us thy peace.

According to the holy institution, example and command of our
Lord Jesus Christ, and for a memorial of him, we do this:
who, the same night in which he was betrayed took bread
   (*here the minister shall take the bread*)
and when he had blessed, and given thanks, he brake it
   (*here he shall break the bread*)
and said:
   'Take, eat; this is my body, which is broken for you:
   This do in remembrance of me.'
   (*here the minister shall communicate himself and the
   two elders*)

After the same manner also, he took the cup
   (*here he shall raise the cup*)
saying:
      'This cup is the new covenant in my blood:
      This do ye, as oft as ye drink it,
      in remembrance of me!'
   (*here the minister shall communicate himself and the
   two elders*)

      The things of God for the people of God:
      O taste and see that the Lord is good:
      Blessed is the man that trusteth in him.

*　　*　　*

(*When all have received, and all the bread and wine have
been replaced on the table and covered, the minister shall
say:*)
      The peace of the Lord Jesus Christ be with you all.
Let us pray
O Lord God, Father of our Lord Jesus Christ, we thank thee
for this meal in which we have shared; and we thank thee for
thy faithful promise to thy children, that in all their ways
thy hand is strong to stay them and thy strength is sure: as
we have received, so let us give: send us into thy world
ready to serve; send us into the dark corners of life, bearing
thy light: send us to bless, and to bring justice: fed at
thy table, send us to thy fields, white unto harvest: for-

given and set free, send us to liberate: found here, send us
to find our true selves, and to help others to find thee, true
God and faithful Father of all.

> Go: serve the Lord: you are free:
> and the blessing of God Almighty,
> the Father, the Son and the Holy Spirit
> be amongst you and remain with you always.
>
> AMEN

9

A SHORT ORDER FOR HOLY COMMUNION

The grace of the Lord Jesus Christ be with you all.

Let us hear again St. Paul's description of how this sacrament
began: 'I received from the Lord (he wrote) what I also delivered
to you, that the Lord Jesus on the night when he was betrayed
took bread, and when he had given thanks, he broke it, and
said, "This is my body which is for you. Do this in remembrance
of me." In the same way also he took the cup, after supper,
saying, "This cup is the new covenant in my blood. Do this
as often as you drink it, in remembrance of me." For as
often as you eat this bread and drink the cup, you proclaim
the Lord's death until he comes.'

Let us then do as he said, in word and action. As the Lord
Jesus took bread, so we take this bread and wine, for his
use and ours in sacrament; and as Jesus gave thanks to God,
let us do so also; let us pray.

Prayer
Holy, glorious and blessed God, we praise you for the world
we live in, for the gift of life, and for your providing for
all our needs.

Above all we bless you for coming into this world in Christ
Jesus, made man for us men and for our salvation: for the compassion and healing of his life, the glory of his cross, the
wonder and triumph of his rising, the coming of his kingdom,
and the life-giving presence of his Spirit.

Send your Spirit, to sanctify us and the gifts of bread and
wine which we set upon this table : that the bread which we
break may be to us the communion of the body of Christ, and the
cup which we bless the communion of the blood of Christ —
that by this we may remember him, and share in the victory
of his death and resurrection.

Lord, we remember here the world we live in, in its suffering
and conflict, its hunger and sorrow . . .
> the nation we belong to, in its tension and striving,
> the city where we live, and our leaders and fellow-
> citizens . . .
> the Church, sent out into this world to heal and to
> help . . .
> the congregation we represent here, with its heritage
> and its future, its young people and its old people,
> its scattered homes, and especially any where there
> is illness, or trouble, or sorrow . . .

We offer our thanksgiving, our thought for others, and our
own selves for service, as we say together the prayer Jesus
taught:
OUR FATHER . . . . . .

The Lord Jesus, on the night when he was betrayed, took bread,
and when he had given thanks, he broke it, and said: 'This is
my body which is for you, do this in remembrance of me.'

In the same way he took the cup, saying: 'This cup is the new
covenant sealed by my blood. Whenever you drink it, do this
in remembrance of me.'

(*Distribution of the bread*)
Take this and eat it: this is the body of Christ, which is
for you. Do this in remembrance of him . . .

(*Distribution of the cup*)
This cup is the new covenant, sealed by Christ's blood, which
was shed so that the sins of many might be forgiven. Drink
from it . . .

(*Here, or above*)
The things of God for the people of God!

Prayers
Thanks be to God . . . for the word he has spoken . . .
the way he has shown . . . the burden he has lifted . . .
the question he has answered . . . the communion he has created . . .
the memories he has evoked of those who have passed into his
eternal keeping . . .
As you have bid us come, Lord, so now send us out to live in
Christ:

> Christ be with me, Christ within me,
> Christ behind me, Christ before me,
> Christ beside me, Christ to win me,
> Christ to comfort and restore me,
> Christ beneath me, Christ above me,
> Christ in quiet, Christ in danger,
> Christ in heart of all that love me,
> Christ in mouth of friend and stranger. (*St. Patrick*)

And to him be glory for ever . . .

OR
Lord God, we give thanks . . . for a prayer answered . . .
for a problem made clearer . . . for hope awakened . . .
for faith made stronger . . . for grace bestowed . . .
for a blessing to take away . . .
Join our thanksgiving to that of other worshippers in other
places, in sanctuaries near and far, in places of rejoicing,
of testing, of danger, of challenge . . . and to that of those
whom you have lifted beyond this life to eternity, the ran-
somed and the redeemed of all ages, and the beloved of our
own hearts.
Cheer us on our way by the memory and the company of all these,
and bring us at last to our rejoicing; and to you be glory,
O God, Father, Son and Holy Spirit, for ever.

OR
Gracious God, we say a blessing for a Father's gifts, and we
go away to live by them, at home and at work.
Grant us to see in every family table an image of the communion table; to see in all the daily bread shared at home
the sign of your providing and protecting; and to carry into
all our converse, at home and with friends, something of
the fellowship of the Church.
And unite us in the Spirit here and everywhere with the rest
of your family, divided from us by distance, or by death —
until the day of our last homecoming to you; through Christ
Jesus our Lord, to whom be glory.

10

A FOLK COMMUNION

To Guitar Accompaniment, as celebrated in Iona Abbey

(The Hymn prior to the Great Prayer was 'Lord of the Dance'

(*Where guitars are used to accompany a corporate act of
worship, it is advisable that all the acts of praise, including
introductory and recessional music, should be confined to the
hymns and compositions which belong to the medium of strii*

Call to prayer
When the cloud covers the mercy seat, look down on thy peo
O God, and speak peace.

Prayer
Almighty God, Creator, the morning is yours, rising to fullne
The summer is yours, dipping into autumn. Eternity is yours,
dipping into time.
The vibrant grasses, the scent of flowers, the lichen on the

rocks, the tang of sea-weed, all are yours. Here in this
luxurious land we live in a garden of your creating.

But Creation is not enough: always in the beauty the fore-
shadowing of decay. Lambs once frolicking, now grown sheep,
led off to slaughter. Nature red as well as green. In the
garden also, always the thorn. Creation is not enough.

Almighty God, Redeemer, the sap of life in our bones and
being is yours.
But, always in the beauty, the tang of sin in our consciences.
The dry lichen of sins long dead, but scarred upon our minds.
In the garden that is each of us, always the thorn.

Yet all are yours. Not only the lives you have given, but
also our sins that you have taken . . . even our livid rebel-
lions that you have lifted and nailed to the Cross, all are
yours. Our redemption is enough and we are free.

Holy Spirit, Giver of Life, breathe on us, fill us with life
anew: in that new creation . . . already upon us . . . breaking
through . . . groaning and travailing . . . but breaking through.
When neither morning or noon, spring or autumn shall be any
more . . . sheep shall not be led to slaughter . . . even the
thorn shall disappear, and the whole earth shall cry 'Glory'
at the marriage feast of the Lamb.
In this new creation, already upon us, fill us with life anew.

You are admitting us now into a wonderful communion, the fore-
taste of that final feast.
Help us to put on the wedding garment —
By the glory of your creation around us, by the assurance of
your forgiveness within us, by the wind of your spirit eddying
within these walls, help us to put on the wedding garment
so that we come glad to the feast.

So shall we go out into the world, as servants of Christ the
King, to whom, with you O Spirit, and with the Father be glory
for ever.   AMEN

Sermon   Offering   The Creed

LORD OF THE DANCE

The words of the Institution

THE ACTION PRAYER

Lift up your hearts.
We lift them up to the Lord.

Let us give thanks to our Lord God.
It is meet and right so to do.

Indeed it is right . . . what else can we do . . . any time . . .
any place . . . than feel uplifted and warmed . . . in our
whole being . . . Father God?
What else can we do than be grateful?
For we remember you, O Christ . . . the Sun behind all suns:

You left your royal throne . . . left the realm of light . . .
to enter our common paths and to grope for us in our darknes
Just for us men . . . common . . . sly . . . and prickly as we are
to lift us and soothe us and make us clean.

We cannot put it into words . . . but we try to say with our
lips what we do believe in our hearts . . . that we really are
so grateful . . . that you were born in poverty and not in
privilege . . . that you joined with evil and with filth . . .
but you never got contaminated.

Lord Jesus . . . mystical presence of love . . . we are so
grateful that (when all your sweetness and forbearance went
for nothing) . . . you still climbed on to a cross, to make us
certain you really meant it all . . .
That for six black hours you danced into outer darkness . . .
with the devil on your back . . .
. . . And that, after three days, up came the sun, King Jesus!

And you walked again with men . . . and spoke . . . and broke
bread again . . . and the dance went on . . . We are so grateful
. . . And how grateful we are that you are walking and speaki
with us now . . . and what you are Lord of is a dance and not
a dirge . . .
So that we too can dance, wherever we may be . . .

So grateful that when everything shall be over, it is a dance
you call us to.

This is not how we ought to thank you but it is the best we
can do . . . to let you know how uplifted we are . . . and
how humbled . . .

Just for a moment we are our real selves . . . as we know
we should always be . . . Therefore with all the powers that
go to make the world, we sing to you . . . with the whole
realm of nature . . . with Columba . . . and Kentigern and
Ninian (who can't really be dead) . . . and with all those who
used to worship with us on earth, our own dear ones, who —
in the mystery — still stand beside us, they in your nearer
presence.

We join with them all, singing in our hearts . . .

> 'Holy, Holy, Holy, Lord God of Hosts . . . Heaven and
> earth are full of your glory . . . Glory be to God on
> high . . . Hosanna in the highest. Blessed is he that
> comes in the name of the Lord.'

And we ask you to look upon us as, in the mystery, we bring
you back. For you are coming to us now, Mystical presence of
Christ. You always do, when anyone calls . . .

You come to us as we grasp that this bread is vibrant with
you (who are Light and Life) and this wine vibrates with you
(dark with your continuing sacrifice).

You are coming to us; so that as we touch all bread and wine,
we know it is you that we touch.

And you enter us . . . binding us together, outwardly . . .
inwardly . . . totally . . . the seal of our right to dance.

It is in this mystery that we pray for

> The Church throughout the world . . . we are embodied
> with them all, now.
>
> The congregation from which we come . . . we are em-
> bodied with them now.
>
> All sick persons known to us and all starving . . .
> we are embodied with them all.
>
> And the people we hate . . . and the people who hate
> us . . . we are embodied with them all, now.

And because you are one with us, make us to be like
you to them.
Healthy things are only for healthy people . . .
and we have been made healthy.
But, dear Lord, how we fail!

*O Lamb of God you take away the sins of the
world, have mercy upon us.
O Lamb of God you take away the sins of the world,
grant us your peace.*

The peace of the Lord Jesus Christ be with us all.
OUR FATHER. . . . . .

Closing Hymn
Short Prayer of Thanksgiving
The Benediction

11

A HOUSE COMMUNION

The Lord Jesus said: 'Where two or three are met together
in my name, I am there among them.'
He invites us to this table, not because we are good, but
because he is generous. He himself asks us to break bread in
this way as a memorial of him, and it is a means of joining
us to him and to each other.

*THE GRACE OF THE LORD JESUS CHRIST
BE WITH US*
In his name I take this bread and this wine for this holy
meal. And let us thank God.

Holy, holy, holy Lord God of all:
Heaven and earth are full of your glory;
Glory be to you, O Lord most high.

68

Lord God, you loved the world so much that you gave your only Son, that everyone who has faith in him may have eternal life.

We praise and thank you for our Saviour and what he means to us. And remembering his love and what he has done for us we make this memorial before you, until he comes again. Make holy, by your Spirit, both us and this bread and wine, that the bread we break may be a means of sharing in the body of Christ, and this cup of blessing a means of sharing in his blood, that we by faith may be made bone of his bone and flesh of his flesh, one with him and one with each other, that the world may know him in us and believe in him.

OUR FATHER . . . . . .

THE FRACTION

Lamb of God, you take away the sin of the world, have mercy on us.
Lamb of God, you take away the sin of the world, give us your peace.
Take this and eat: this is the body of Christ, which is for you: do this as a memorial of him.

This cup is the new covenant sealed by the blood of Christ, which is shed for many for the forgiveness of sins. Drink from it, all of you.

THE PEACE OF THE LORD JESUS CHRIST BE WITH YOU

Heavenly Father, we rejoice that we are made one with our Lord Christ, and that in him we are one with each other and with all who believe in him. We thank you for those who have gone before us in this faith, who though they are dead are alive for ever in Christ Jesus, and so are with us now. Keep us close to you in our life, and bring us at the last to those things which are beyond our seeing and beyond imagining, which you have prepared for those who love you, through Jesus Christ our Lord.

The peace of God, which is beyond our utmost understanding, keep guard over our hearts and our thoughts, in Christ Jesus; and the blessing . . .

12

MARRIAGE SERVICE—FIRST ORDER

(*Praise*)

Our help is in the name of the Lord, maker of heaven
and earth.

and *either*
Unless the Lord builds the house, its builders will have
toiled in vain

or
Jesus said: The Creator made them from the beginning male a
female . . . for this reason a man shall leave his father
and mother, and be made one with his wife; and the two shall
become one flesh.

We have come together, fellow men and women, to witness th
joining of this man and this woman in marriage, and to offer
prayer for them.

As a way of life, marriage is part of God's ordering of his
creation; but, although it is common throughout the world,
the married state is not to be entered upon lightly or care-
lessly, but reverently, seriously, and soberly, with due
consideration of the purposes for which it has been appointed

Marriage is appointed by God for the life-long companionship
help, and comfort which husband and wife ought to have from
each other.
It is appointed to be a healthy and holy setting for the
expression of the natural instincts and affections which God
has implanted within us.
It is appointed that children may be born and brought up in
families, to the glory of God.
And it is appointed for the welfare of human society for whic
the honouring of the marriage bond provides a firm foundati

Christian marriage, moreover, brings special responsibilities, and, to those who enter it with sincerity of purpose, special grace to meet these responsibilities. Marriages begun with prayer are to be sustained by prayer. The children of such unions are to be brought up to serve and love our Lord. By the quality of their commitment to one another the partners are called upon to be examples of the truth of Paul's declaration that, in its mysterious depth, the relationship of husband and wife may fitly be compared to that of Christ and the Church.

To help towards the attainment of these ends, we believe that our Lord is present, here and always, in the power of his Holy Spirit, as, we read in Holy Scripture, he was present in the days of his earthly life to bless a marriage at Cana in Galilee.

Into this profound and lasting relationship these two persons now desire to enter. If anyone can show any good reason why they may not lawfully be joined together, let him now declare it.

Also I require and charge you both, remembering that you are answerable to God, that if either of you know any good reason why you may not lawfully be joined in marriage, you confess it now.

Since no objection has been made, let us ask for God's blessing on the union now to be formed.

Let us pray:
Almighty God, Father of us all, we turn to you, the giver of all good things, and humbly thank you for all the blessings of our life. Especially at this time we give thanks for love — for the love and concern of parents and all who have taught, guided, and cared for us through the years; and for the love and trust with which these, your children, come together now. We thank you, too, that you have appointed marriage to guard, to strengthen, and to make perfect that same gift of love. And since we believe that it is only with your help that we can do anything well, we ask for those now before you the

71

gift of the Holy Spirit that in sincerity and truth they may make and keep their vows; and this we ask through Jesus Christ our Lord.

(*Congregation stands*)

A . . . . . . and B . . . . . ., as a seal to the vows you are about to make, you will give to each other the right hand.

(*Man*): I, ..., take you, ..., / to be my wedded wife; / and do, / in the presence of God / and before this congregation (*or* these witnesses), / promise and covenant / to be a loving, faithful, and dutiful husband to you, / until God shall separate us by death.

(*Woman*): I, ...,take you, ..., / to be my wedded husband; and do, / in the presence of God / and before this congregation (*or* these witnesses), / promise and covenant / to be a loving, faithful, and dutiful wife to you, / until God shall separate us by death.

God has heard these vows, and we are witnesses of them.

(*Ring is placed in book*)
Bless this ring, O merciful Lord, that he who gives it and she who wears it may continue faithful, the one to the other, in unbroken love

or
Bless these rings, O merciful Lord, that being given and received they may be signs of continuing faithfulness and unbroken love.

(*Groom places ring on bride's finger (and vice versa*))
As a visible sign of your commitment to one another this ring is (these rings are) given and received. By this sign you take each other, to have and to hold from this day forward, for better, for worse; for richer, for poorer; in sickness and in health; to love and to cherish, till death do you part.

(*Bride and groom again join right hands*)
By the authority committed to me as a minister in the Church of Jesus Christ, and having heard you exchange your vows of love and faithfulness, I pronounce you to be husband and wife

(*here the minister places his right hand on the joined hands of the couple*) In the Name of the Father, and of the Son, and of the Holy Spirit.   AMEN

Our Lord has said: What God has joined together, let no man put asunder.

(*Bride and groom kneel*)
The Lord sanctify and bless you. The Lord pour out the riches of his grace upon you, that you may please him, and live together in holy love until your lives' end.
and/or The Aaronic Blessing.

(*Bride and groom rise; congregation is seated*)
That love which draws a man and a woman together in marriage is both physical and spiritual.
We read now from the Bible part of the love poems to be found in the Song of Solomon — poems which give expression to the physical attraction of a man and a woman towards each other.
A bridegroom speaks first:
You have ravished my heart, my sister, my bride,
    you have ravished my heart with a glance of your eyes,
    with one jewel of your necklace.
How sweet is your love, my sister, my bride!
    how much better is your love than wine,
    and the fragrance of your oils than any spice!
Your lips distil nectar, my bride;
    honey and milk are under your tongue;
    the scent of your garments is like the scent of
    Lebanon . . .
Set me as a seal upon your heart,
    as a seal upon your arm;
for love is strong as death,
    jealousy is cruel as the grave.
Its flashes are flashes of fire,
    a most vehement flame.
Many waters cannot quench love,
    neither can floods drown it.

And his bride speaks:
> As an apple tree among the trees of the wood,
> so is my beloved among young men.
> With great delight I sat in his shadow
> and his fruit was sweet to my taste.
> He brought me to the banqueting house,
> and his banner over me was love.
> Sustain me with raisins,
> refresh me with apples;
> for I am sick with love.
> O that his left hand were under my head,
> and that his right hand embraced me! . . .
> The voice of my beloved!
> Behold, he comes . . .
> My beloved is mine and I am his.

St. Paul describes the more spiritual side of love in his first
letter to the Corinthians, where he writes:
(Here read 1 Cor. 13:4-8a, 13 in N.E.B.)
*(Or, in place of the foregoing, Psalm 127 or 128 and (part
of) Eph. 5:21-33 or (part of) 1 John 4:7-18 or 1
Cor. 7:2-4.)*

Hear also the gracious words of our Lord.

(John 15:9-13)
(If Bible is presented): Take this book and on its
wisdom build your home.

Let us pray:
Most holy and merciful God, by whom the solitary are set in
families, we pray that your blessing may remain with A . . . . . .
and B . . . . . ., now joined together in your Name. May their
marriage be for them a source of great and lasting good.
Spare them long to each other, and keep them faithful, tender
and true, so that they may live together in peace and holiness.
Bless them in their home and in all the works of their hands,
supplying their needs and defending them from all that would
harm. In prosperity may they be grateful to you, the Giver
of all good: in trouble may they find that you are their refuge

and their strength. So lead them through this life, we pray,
that when they have fully served you in their generation,
they may be received into the presence of your glory, and be
numbered with those who are called to the marriage supper of
the Lamb, who is Jesus Christ our Lord, in whose prevailing
words we further pray and say: OUR FATHER . . . . . .

or

O gracious and merciful Father, by whose appointment marriage
has been given to the human race, and by whose blessing it is
strengthened and sustained, we pray for . . . . . . and . . . . . .,
now joined as husband and wife. Keep them loyal and steadfast
to each other. May their love know no doubt or change, but
may shared tasks, trials, and joys bind them ever more closely
in heart.

O God, whose Son, Jesus Christ, shared at Nazareth the life
of an earthly home, we pray that he may be acknowledged as
head of the household of these your children. And, as he found
his authority in serving, so may they learn to serve one another in love. We remember, too, the homes from which they
have come, and pray that you will bless those who have given
them to each other.

O God, by whom, in the Gospel, we are all invited to the marriage
supper of your Son, so incline the hearts of these your servants
that they may give obedience to your call. Bring them, at
the end of their days to your banqueting house, and may your
banner over them be always love; through Jesus Christ our
Lord in whose prevailing words we further pray and say:
OUR FATHER . . . . . .

(Praise)

The peace of God which passes all understanding, keep your
hearts and minds in the knowledge and love of God, and of his
Son Jesus Christ our Lord; and the blessing of God almighty,
the Father, the Son, and the Holy Spirit, be amongst you, and
remain with you always.   AMEN

13

MARRIAGE SERVICE—SECOND ORDER

Note

The Marriage Service contains a large element of ritual,
and we commonly surround it with secular rituals – veils, dresses,
cake-cutting, etc. One must do justice to the ritual element
in the service while wanting to ensure that what is expressed
is reality. This is an attempt to translate the marriage service into English which is reasonably natural, comprehensible
and personal and yet retains something of the dignity and
formality of the ritual occasion. For this reason some of the
more familiar traditional language has been retained. The
structure of the *Book of Common Order* 1940, has been retained,
help has been received from the *Book of Common Order* 1928,
Prayers for Divine Service (1929) and *Contemporary Prayers for
Public Worship* (S.C.M.).

The prayers in this service are given only as examples: they
were appropriate to one particular marriage, but might not be
appropriate to others.

But the same may be said of the whole service, which is
presented only as an example, and to encourage others who are
seeking a more satisfactory service.

*   *   *

If the service begins with a hymn (such as 'Praise to
the Lord, the Almighty'. R.C.H. 22) the bride may
enter during the singing, or the hymn may be sung
after all have taken their places.

Then the minister says:
Unless the Lord builds the house, those who build it labour
in vain.
Our help is in the name of the Lord, who made heaven and
earth.

Dear friends, we have come together in God's presence and as his congregation in order that A . . . . . . B . . . . . . and L . . . . . . M . . . . . . may be joined in marriage.

Marriage is a state of life which we believe God himself has provided and instituted for his children. Jesus, our Lord, blessed it by his presence as a wedding-guest at the marriage in Cana of Galilee. In the New Testament marriage is commended as honourable in all, and the marriage union is seen as a symbol of the union of loyalty and love that exists between Christ and his people.

It is, therefore, not something to be undertaken lightly or unadvisedly, but thoughtfully and reverently and as before God, and with due consideration of the reasons for which it was given us.

It was given us for the sake of the life-long companionship, help and comfort that husband and wife ought to have of each other.

It was given us so that family life may continue, and that children may be brought up in the love and security of a stable and happy home.

It was given us for the welfare of human society, which tends to be strong and happy only where the marriage commitment is kept and honoured.

Into this relationship A . . . . . . and L . . . . . . now wish to enter. So if anyone can show any good reason why their marriage would not be lawful, let him speak now, or for ever hold his peace.

Since no one speaks against it, let us ask God's blessing on what we are about to do in his name.

Let us pray
O God our Father, gracious and loving God, we thy children, who are not worthy of the least of thy mercies, pour out our thanks and our praise when we consider how rich is thy providing, how good are the gifts of thy grace.

We thank thee for all human happiness, and especially at this time for the institution of marriage, which thou hast given

us to guard and enclose, to nourish and perfect thine own gift
of love.

We thank thee for these thy children, who stand before us and
before thee today. We thank thee for the goodness to the homes
from which they come, for the joy which they themselves have
given to these homes, and for the love and affection in which
they have been, and are, upheld by families and friends.

We thank thee for the joy which they have found in one another,
for friendship deepening into love, and love deepening into
certainty and trust as they commit themselves to one another
in marriage.

And since without thy help we cannot and we would not go, we
pray that as by thy providence they have been brought to this
hour, in it they may be filled with thy grace.

May they be as conscious of thy presence as they are of ours,
and enter into marriage as in thy sight, confident that they
are indeed under thy blessing, and trusting in thee to prosper
and establish what thou hast begun.
Through Jesus Christ our Lord.   AMEN

Will the congregation please stand?

A . . . . . . and L . . . . . ., as a seal to the vows that you are
now to make, will you give each other the right hand?

(*Then the Bridegroom and Bride make their vows to one another,
turning a little towards one another and reading the vows
from a card held by the minister.*)

The Bridegroom:
I, A . . . . . ., take you, L . . . . . .
to be my wedded wife,
and, in the presence of God and before this congregation,
I promise and covenant
to be a loving, faithful, and dutiful husband to you,
until we shall be separated by death.

The Bride:
I, L . . . . . ., take you, A . . . . . .
to be my wedded husband,
and in the presence of God and before this congregation,

I promise and covenant
to be a loving, faithful, and dutiful wife to you,
until we shall be separated by death.

Then the minister says:
As a token of the covenant into which you have entered, this
ring is given and received.

By this sign you take each other, to have and to hold from
this day forward, for better, for worse, for richer, for
poorer, in sickness and in health, to love and to cherish,
till death do you part.

Inasmuch as you have made your covenant together in marriage
publicly declaring it before God and these witnesses, I
pronounce you to be husband and wife, in the name of the
Father and of the Son and of the Holy Spirit.   AMEN

What God has joined together man must not separate.

(The couple kneel for the blessing)

The Lord bless you and keep you
the Lord make his face to shine upon you
and be gracious unto you.
The Lord lift up his countenance upon you
and give you peace, both now and evermore.   AMEN

A Hymn or a Psalm such as Ps. 89, 15-18, may be sung then.
'O greatly bless'd the people are'

Then the minister says:
In the New Testament we read of the love which Christians
ought to have to one another, and of the joy which they find
in one another and in God.

Hear the Word of God.
1 Corinthians 13, 4-7, 13.
1 John 4, 7-12, 16b.

and the words of Jesus in the Gospel according to St. John,
Ch. 15, 7-13.

*(After the readings the minister preaches a short sermon
or addresses the couple in words suitable to the occasion,
and then calls the congregation to prayer:)*

O Lord our God, author and giver of all good things, who
hast set the solitary in families, that through the love
that has surrounded us we may become free to love and serve
others; we pray for these thy children who have been joined
together in marriage: that as they have been richly blessed
in love, so they may richly bless one another and all who
know them. Grant that they may dwell in unity and love all
the days of their life, seeking one another's welfare, bearing
one another's burdens, sharing one another's joys. May they
grow continually in freedom and in faith, enriched and
drawn closer by all the experiences of life. (Bless their
love with children.) Free them from worldly anxieties that
they may have time and love to spare for those who are in
trouble or in need. Above all, heavenly Father, we pray that
at all times they may know thy presence, thy power, thy joy
and peace, until they come to thine eternal kingdom.
Through Jesus Christ our Lord who taught us when we pray to
say:
OUR FATHER......

Then, after a Hymn or Psalm of Praise, the service closes
with a Benediction.

14

MARRIAGE SERVICE—THIRD ORDER

Unless it is the Lord who builds a home, those who
build it work in vain
So let us worship God.

PRAISE

Preamble:
My friends, we are here, as God's family
so that A...... and B......
may be united in Christian marriage.

80

A true marriage originates in God's plan for our lives.
It is our Heavenly Father who made us male and female,
and who ordained that we should leave our parental homes,
to become one flesh.

We can only be married, in the fullest sense,
if in all our preparations for marriage,
and in this service in particular
We are seeking his will for our lives,
 seeking his blessing upon all we do and plan
 seeking his Spirit of love to purify and complete
 our earthly loves.

The Word of God gives us three objectives for marriage:

1. The lifelong companionship of husband and wife . . .
   'what God has joined together, let not man put
   asunder.'
2. That children may be brought into the world, and
   may grow up in a Christian home, to know and
   love God.
3. That human society may be enriched, for where
   marriage is debased, the whole structure of
   society crumbles.

A . . . . . . and B . . . . . . have expressed their wish to enter
into marriage as Christian people, before God, and before the
family of God,
so let us seek God's presence in our midst,
 let us thank him for his goodness,
 let us admit to our sins,
 and let us seek his grace to make this service a reality.
 Let us pray to God, the giver of life and of love, our
Father.

Prayer:
O Lord Our God, How wonderful is life!
 How rich its variety of joy and sorrow!
 How precious are the lives of those dear to us!

But life is *your* gift,
In everything that makes life worth living, it's you we see
at work.
In every human life we see something of you
And, in the end, it's only in you that our lives make sense.
O Father in Heaven we praise you for the gift of life!

O Lord our God, How glorious is love!
    How wonderful are the various aspects of love we've
    seen,
       in the parents who brought us into this world . . .
       in the family and friends who have cared for us,
       and especially today we rejoice in the love you've
       set between A . . . . . . and B . . . . . .

But love is your presence,
It's you we know, when we know love,
It's you we see reflected in everybody who loves us,
It's you whose love will never let us go.
O Father in Heaven, we praise you for the gift of love!

May life and love pour into our lives now . . .
light up all that we are doing with a new glory,
so that we may know your presence.

O forgive us that we've so often taken life and love for
granted!
that we have selfishly misused what you gave us,
and have hurt those who love us . . . have hurt you, dear Lord.

This day, may life and love be renewed in us all,
and especially in A . . . . . . and in B . . . . . .
so that the love that joins their lives together
may be truly your spirit working through them.

May it be your love that enables them to take their vows,
and to keep them for the rest of their lives,
All this we ask because of what you've shown us of yourself
in Jesus Christ Our Lord.　　AMEN

The Vows
Before God and this congregation
I A . . . . . . take you, B . . . . . .
to be my wedded wife.
I promise and covenant
to be a loving, faithful and dutiful husband to you
till death shall part us.

Before God and this congregation
I, B . . . . . . take you, A . . . . . .
to be my wedded husband.
I promise and covenant
to be a loving, faithful and dutiful wife to you
till death shall part us.

The ring:
By this covenant you have made before God and before his people
you have bound yourselves to live together as husband and
wife, and as a token of that covenant this ring (these rings)
is (are) given and received.

Let this be the outward expression of the holy love that binds
you, that giving and receiving you may be united by the Lord
himself, sharing all that lies before you
for better or for worse, for richer or for poorer, in sickness
or in health,
to love and to cherish until death shall part you.

In the light of the love that led you here,
and of the covenant you have made before God and before his
people
I declare you to be husband and wife,
In the name of the Father and of the Son and of the Holy Spirit.
AMEN

The Blessing:
And now, as you first act together as husband and wife
receive the blessing of God.

> May the love of God unite you
> the joy of God fill your hearts
> the peace of God rest upon the home you set up,

and the strength of God equip you both to serve him
together,
In the name of the Father and of the Son and of the
Holy Spirit,   AMEN

The Word of God:
Now, stand up before God,
Face the future with courage,
Hear the Word of God to you,
For it is the only sure foundation upon which to build up
your home-life in a world so full of storms and strife
and in the face of your own human weakness.

So listen to what St. John tells us of the real nature of
love — 1 John 4:7.
And hear what the Lord himself has to say to you in the
Gospel — John 15:9.

Let us pray
O living God,
We thank you for showing us just how you love us by living
out a human life in this world.
We thank you for showing us that your love in a human body
can stand up to temptation,
can master suffering,
and can even conquer death itself.
May A . . . . . . and B . . . . . .dwell in this love,
May this love dwell in them,
so that your joy may be in them . . . and their joy be complete

May it be your love that is the true foundation of their home,
that it may be firmly rooted and grounded in love.
May it be your love that is the true light of their home,
that everybody who enters it may see something of
you in it.
May it be your love that is their true treasure and wealth,
that their happiness may not depend on outward
circumstances.
So may their home be a sanctuary of your love,

84

making them a blessing to neighbours, friends, family,
and to all the generations that follow.

When all goes well with them and their cup of happiness over-
flows shield them lest they take their blessings for granted,
When they face problems, guide them by your spirit that they
may find your way through.
When they come to suffering and to sorrow, may they be drawn
closer together, and closer to you.
And so, through green pastures and through dark valleys alike
may their journey through life be a journey into God led at
each step by the good shepherd.

And what we ask for these your servants, Father, we ask for
each family represented here today:
that those who pledged love to each other long ago
may find their love deepened today,
that those who took vows to each other long ago,
may renew those vows today,
that new love may radiate out from each life creating
new joy and new strength.
And it is as one family we join together to pray:
OUR FATHER . . . . . .

Praise

Blessing:

Go in peace

Be joyful in the love of God
And the blessing of God
Father, Son and Holy Spirit
be upon you all this day and for ever.   AMEN

15

FUNERAL SERVICE—FIRST ORDER

Let us hear the living words of scripture.
The souls of the righteous are in the hands of God.
There shall no torment touch them , they are in peace.
The eternal God is their refuge; underneath are the
everlasting arms.

Christ is risen, as he said.
Death hath no more dominion over him.
The stone which the builders rejected is become the head
of the corner.
This is the Lord's doing: and it is marvellous in our eyes.
Wherefore let us reckon ourselves to be dead unto sin:
but alive unto God in Christ Jesus.

Prayer
Heavenly Father you are all about us:
       and you are all about him.
You love us with an everlasting love:
       without any shadow cast by turning.
Only as you now give us faith to believe this,
       can you turn the shadow of death into morning.
Give us Easter faith, while it is still dark!

Help each one of us to hear you call us by name,
       while it is still dark!
Enable us, even in our rebellion, to call you Master still.

So shall we hear your word . . . not as a tale that is told,
       but as vibrant speech.
So shall our company here . . . neither listless nor becalmed . .
Be lifted back on to the wave of faith,
       to brave, with him, in you, another cruise.
Abolish time, Lord, and speak to us through your word.   AN

Readings
Psalm 23. Psalm 103:8-18. 1 Corinthians 15:53-58.
John 14:1-6.

Prayer
Lord God you have not set your love upon us because we are a
great people, because we are indeed the least of all people.

But you have set your love upon us because you love us.

Thus awed and abased, we are exalted, uplifted, enabled to
thank you for that death that abolished death, and for the
splendour of that resurrection that has opened the gates
for us . . . even for us . . . even for now.

For we too are already dead and our lives are hid with Christ,
in you. We too are already buried with Christ in baptism, and
so risen with Christ to newness of life.

For us too the undertaker has already been and gone.

Our citizenship is already in heaven. We are but ambassadors
in this alien land of earth, capable of redemption though it be.

It is in this consciousness and this appropriation that we
pray for those who mourn.

For those of this household . . .

For any unable to be present, whose thoughts are towards this
house at this same hour . . . especially those who worked with
him in days gone by, and loved his strictness and were
devoted to his purposes.

Come very near beside all these, shepherding Lord, and guide
them in the darkness. We ask it in faith.

O God, before your face the generations rise and pass away.
But your Empire stands secure, and its bounds increase.
We bless you for all your servants departed in the faith;
especially our dear ones gone forward who, at such an hour
as this, come very near to us.

Tell them how we love them, and miss them, and long for the
day when we shall meet with them again.

Especially we thank you for your servant J . . . . . .
(*Here follow personal details*)

87

By the spirit of the just made perfect, teach us in our turn,
O Lord, to give and not to count the cost: to fight and not
to heed the wounds: to labour and to seek for no reward save
only the knowledge that we do your will. For only so shall
we be worthy of those great souls who, in every age, have
ventured all in obedience to your call: of whom this world
has never been worthy, but for whom all the trumpets have
sounded on the other side.
Through Jesus Christ our Lord.

And the grace of the Lord Jesus Christ, and the love of God
and the fellowship of the Holy Spirit, be with you all.

AMEN

16

FUNERAL SERVICE—SECOND ORDER

Beloved, we have come together today to give thanks
for the life of A . . . . . . B . . . . . . (*Here may follow a brief
personal reference*)
We shall remember him with joy as a vital living presence, and
true friend.
We shall remember him with pride as a fine workman, and a
courageous patient.
We shall remember him with gratitude as a loyal colleague,
and a loving relative.

Thus hand in hand with our sense of loss and sorrow goes an
awareness of great gain; for it is people like A . . . . . . B . . . . . .
who bring friendship, human warmth, and quiet good humour
into a world that is all too short of them

or
He had no near kin, but we have come here to show that he was
part of our family, the one family of man, the household of
God.

We meet together today in the conviction that death is not a calamity, but is an event we can face without fear, or bitterness, or guilt.

We believe that those who have died are at rest,
and that the promise is true that no evil shall touch them.

We want C . . . . . . D . . . . . . and all the other members of the family circle to know that their loss is our loss, their sorrow our sorrow, and their strength our continuing love and friendship.
That faith and trust is reflected in the praise we now sing.

(*Here follows an appropriate hymn or psalm*)
Readings: 'The Lord is my shepherd . . .'

(Psalm 23. A.V.)

or

'If I lift up my eyes to the hills . . .'

(Psalm 121. N.E.B.)

or

'Then what can separate us from the love of Christ
. . . Jesus our Lord.'   (Rom. 8:35-39. N.E.B.)

or

'Then I saw a new heaven and a new earth
. . . shall be my son.'   (Rev. 21:1-7. N.E.B.)

And as he faced this our death Jesus said to his disciples:
        'Let not your heart be troubled
        . . . neither let it be afraid'   (John 14:1-27. A.V.)

Prayers before Committal
Lord of our lives, as we come together in a sense of common loss and personal grief let the spirit of faith, and love, and compassion so draw us closer together that gradually our fears may be dispelled, our loneliness eased, our hurt healed, and our hope re-kindled. May our natural sorrow rest ever more surely in that deep and quiet confidence which knows that death is not the end, but rather the completion of our lives. And so may we emerge from these dark days to live our lives gently with others in faith and trust and new hope.

Lord, we give thanks for all our friends and loved ones in whom we have seen the light of your presence, and the graciousness of your spirit, and the warmth of your love.

Especially today we give thanks for A . . . . . . B . . . . . . We acknowledge with gladness that ever gracious love of God which with the gift of life freely gave also the greater gift of acceptance — that love incarnated in the lives of parents and family, friends and associates, which surrounded him in infancy, bore with him in adolescence and sustained him in manhood. We are deeply grateful for all he was to those in the close family circle as a husband, brother, and a friend, and a relative. We are glad for all that his wisdom and judgement, his sincerity and company meant to those in business, in pleasure, and in the service of the kingdom. Lord, we shall miss him as long as we live. And yet because his tolerance and energy, his intensity of living and kindliness of feeling, his steadfastness and humour, were so freely given to us, his spirit will always be alive in us, and his memory treasured in our conversation. Lord, the love, loyalty, and respect which lie deep in our hearts cannot be broken or diminished by the passing of time.

Lord, help us to see death for what it really is —
> the end of poverty and the beginning of riches,
> the end of frustration and the beginning of fulfilment,
> the end of fear and the beginning of tranquillity,
> the end of pain and the beginning of joy,
> the end of weakness and the beginning of strength.

O Lord Jesus, whose rich and unforgettable life was lived in the faith that the love which surrounds us is as real and dependable as that of a father, let that same sense of trust and hope steady us at this time.

Let not grief overwhelm us, or a sense of loss embitter us. But out of our sadness let there arise a new joy for so much given to us.

Help us to see that what we love becomes a part of us interfused with our lives, blended with mind and memory, hallowed for ever within our soul. Let not grief take away our hope, or bereavement blind us to what always remains good and lovely and indestructible.

O gracious spirit of peace, come alive within our experience and hurt, within our sorrow and isolation, within the sadness of today and the loneliness of tomorrow. Come alive as the peace and trust which nothing in life or death can kill. Cast out our fears and let not our hearts be troubled, knowing that this world this remains our Father's house. These our prayers we offer through Christ our Lord.   AMEN

The Committal
Here is a promise that we may trust completely: As far as the east is from the west so far has he removed our transgressions from us.

Him that cometh to Me I will in no wise cast out.

In now committing the body of A . . . . . . B . . . . . . (to this hallowed ground) we do so with deep reverence, for that body is the temple during life of a unique and beloved personality. That body now returns to the earth from which it came purified and for ever hallowed; but that spirit lives on.

They shall never again feel hunger or thirst, the sun shall not beat on them (nor any scorching heat) because the Lamb who is at the heart of the throne will be their shepherd, and guide them to the springs of the water of life, and God shall wipe away all tears from their eyes.

The peace of God has come to him.

Prayers after Committal
O Lord Jesus, whose life was lived in the quiet conviction that there is nothing in life that need terrify us, and nothing in death to make us afraid.

We remember with concern those whose sense of loss is keenest at this time because their love was deepest and most personal. As they grieve may they be aware that they do not do so alone. And let regrets give way to gratitude, sorrow be transformed by hope, and a sense of loss grow to a deep thankfulness for

what can never be lost or tarnished. Let not their mourning
be as endless grief, but as the courage of faith and the
prelude to fresh meaning in life. Keep them from bitterness
and self-pity, so that without any disloyalty life may again
blossom as the rose.

Lord, we remember with tenderness those who mourn. Help them
to keep in loving remembrance him who has gone on before, him who
has stood by in times of success and adversity, whose presence
has given so many years of happiness. Help them still to hold
their heads high lest the loss of special friendships sour
their loneliness, and spoil that memory.

And now, Lord, give us all grace to turn back again to life's
tasks with steady nerves, a calm heart, and a courageous
faith, that we may be truly worthy of those who have enriched
our lives beyond measure, and lived in that spirit which
alone can save the world, even the spirit of Him who taught
us to say: 'Our Father . . . . . .'

CLOSING PRAISE, if desired.

Bear ye one another's burdens, and so fulfil the law of Christ.
Thus you will experience the grace bestowed by the Lord Jesus,
the love God offers, and the fellowships the Holy Spirit creates.

AMEN

or
And now may courage, serenity, and all God's other gifts to
his children be yours.
The blessing of God as Father, Son, and Holy Spirit be with
you all.   AMEN

17

SERVICE FOR THE CREMATORIUM— FIRST ORDER

Standing with the Principal Mourners:
We have come here today, your friends and relatives, because
we share with you your sadness and loss at the death of
A . . . . . . B . . . . . .
We want to give more than expressions of consolation and
sympathy, we want to give expression to our faith and to our
living hope, for we believe in God, and that his purposes
will always in the end finally triumph. We therefore know
that death is not the end.
Let us, in that knowledge, worship God.

At the Lectern:
Praise:

God is Love. True love does not die or fade away.It lasts
through pain and difficult times. Bonds of love hold you and
yours together, even now, and for ever. And God is love —
which lives and cannot die.
May God be with you and with your dear one.

Jesus said; 'How blest are those who know their need of God,
the kingdom of God is theirs. How blest are the sorrowful,
they shall find consolation.'

Let us pray:
Great God, we know you in life as the powerful Creator and as
the loving Father.
In your strength the shadow of death can be turned to the
brightness of a new morning.
In your love the silence of this hour can speak to our lonely
and sad hearts. Almighty, and all-loving God we turn to you
now, and to your Word, that we may renew our trust and our
hope; that both we and he/she whom we mourn may be lifted from

the darkness and distress into the light and peace of your presence, for our prayer is through Jesus Christ your Son,

AMEN

From God's Word we express our trust in him:
(*A reading such as Psalm 23 or 121.*)
It is difficult to have such trust in moments like these, but hear now these words of hope — Jesus' words: (*perhaps John 14:1-4, 25-29, and 1.*)
or
Paul's words: (*Romans 8:31-39*)
Finally let us express our confidence in God and in his ways with us:
(*A reading such as 1 Cor. 15:19-26, 55-57; or Rev. 7:9-17; or Rev. 21:1-4 and 22:3-5.*)
Let us pray: (*having intimated to the attendant that the committal will be within this prayer.*)

Lord God, gathered here today, we renew our thanks and praise for all you have done for us through Jesus Christ: that by giving him to live and to die for us you have made known your ways with men and women; you have shown that your love has no limit; that the grave is no end but the gateway to a fuller life in you.

Lord God, many have known the bitterness and the fear of death fade away through the trust and confidence in their faith, so be with us we pray, and still our troubled thoughts.

We give thanks for the life of A . . . . . . B . . . . . . For what he/she has meant and will always mean to us as . . . . . .
(*mentioning the different relationships and activities, as well as the qualities and characteristics of the deceased.*)

We have much to give thanks for in these memories we will treasure as the days pass to years and as the years roll on.

We who have much to give thanks for, and much in our own experience to strengthen us in the faith commend A . . . . . . B . . into God's eternal presence and his sure keeping.

O God, our Heavenly Father, not through human merit do we do this, but in simple trust of your ways with us: your great mercy; your forgiveness of all that would prevent communion;

your love which welcomes us, even as we are, into your
presence.
And so, now that the earthly life of our brother/sister has
come to an end we commit his/her body to be dissolved confident
of the resurrection to eternal life through Jesus Christ our
Lord.

> 'Come to me, all whose work is hard, whose load
> is heavy; and I will give you relief.' (Matt. 11:28.)
> 'I will be your shepherd and guide you to the
> springs of the water of life, and God will wipe all
> tears from your eyes.' (*cf.* Rev. 7:17.)

Comfort us in this faith, O Lord.

And we who are gathered with the family pray for them that
they may be comforted in their sorrow, that the bonds of love
which bind the family may be strength to them, that they
may be content to release their lost one to you, that the
shadows will lift with the assurance that he/she is safe, and
happy, and complete.
Surround all who mourn this day with your continuing compassion. Spare us the selfishness of living in the past.
Teach us to live our lives in the present and for the future,
trusting he/she (*or use name*) will never be far from
us till the day comes when we will all stand before you,
through Jesus Christ our Lord.   AMEN

Praise:

Prayer:
O Lord, our Lord, show us the peace we should seek,
> show us the peace we must try to give,
> show us the peace we can keep,
> show us the peace you have given to us,
and may this peace which is beyond anything we can understand
or reason, keep guard over your hearts and thoughts, and over
your dear ones, now and always.   AMEN

(The final prayer is based on that given on page 108,
Contemporary Prayers for Public Worship; edited by
Caryl Micklem, S.C.M. Press.)

18

SERVICE FOR THE CREMATORIUM—
SECOND ORDER

Opening Praise
Blessed are those who mourn, for they will be comforted

The eternal God is your refuge, and underneath are the ever-lasting arms

The souls of the righteous are in the hand of God, and there no torment will touch them . . . they are in peace

His favour is for a lifetime. Weeping may tarry for the night, but joy comes with the morning

Jesus said: 'I am the Resurrection and the Life. If a man has faith in me, even though he die, he will come to life; and no one who is alive and has faith in me will ever die'

Cast your burden upon the Lord and he will sustain you

Let us pray:
O God our Father, you are a refuge and a strength for us, a helper close at hand in time of distress. Assist us now so to hear the words of our faith that our fears are driven away, our loneliness eased and our hope reawakened. May the Holy Spirit lift us above our natural sorrow into the light and peace of your strengthening presence. Transform the grief of parting and enable us to bear ourselves as those for whom in Christ death is swallowed up in victory, through his strong name we ask it. AMEN

For our strengthening let us read from God's Holy Word . . . .
(*Selections from the following in the New English Bible*)
Psalm 23, Psalm 90:1-6, 10, and 12, Psalm 130, Psalm 121, Romans 8:18, 28, 35-39, 1 Cor. 15:50-58, 1 Thess. 5:1-6, 8-11, 23, Rev. 7:9-17, Rev. 21:1-4 and 22:3-5, St. John 14:1-6, 18-19, 27.

May God add his blessing and comfort to the reading of his
Holy Word and to his name be the glory and the praise.

AMEN

Let us pray:
Dear Father of our Lord Jesus Christ, whose power can work
healing in those whose spirits are shattered, come now and
touch our sadness with thoughts of thanksgiving.
This time would be tragic had not Christ lived and died for
us, revealing the mighty love by which we are surrounded.

This time would be one of despair except that in raising Christ
from the dead you have promised to those who trust him a
share in his resurrection life.

We thank you for the assurance and hope of our faith, and for
those faithful servants whom you have received into your
eternal joy.
But especially we lift our hearts in deepest gratitude for
the life of your servant our brother now parted from our
earthly sight.

Word of special thanksgiving
We thank you for everything in him which reflected your strong
hold of him, and your goodness and loving kindness shed
through his heart and life.
We thank you that having made peace with his maker, he is
forgiven of his sins. We thank you that suffering and weakness
are now over, and that he is reunited with those dear ones
who in past days died in the Lord.
Make it not our grief but our joy to release him to you, in
whose hands we know that he is safe and secure and complete.

Father of mercies and God of all comfort look down, we ask
you, upon all who mourn today with your restoring compassion.
May they not be overcome with sorrow or bitterness or rebellion.
May they and all of us travel more serenely because of today,
and with our eyes set upon Jesus Christ the author and finisher
of our faith may we all walk into the unknown morrow confident
that nothing in life or death can separate us from his love,
and that at the end of our earthly course he will lead us

97

into the blessed life above in the company of all your faithful people, through Jesus Christ our Lord.

Hear these our petitions O God as in the words of Our Lord Jesus Christ we sum up all our prayers saying together: OUR FATHER . . . . . .

The Congregation standing, the minister will say:
Jesus said, 'I am the Resurrection and the Life. If a man has faith in me, even though he die, he shall come to life; and no one who is alive and has faith in me shall ever die.'

THE COMMITTAL

Forasmuch as it has pleased almighty God to take to himself the soul of our brother now departed, we commit his body to be cremated in sure and certain hope of the resurrection to eternal life through our Lord Jesus Christ.

(*After the words of committal the following may be said:*)
I heard a voice from heaven saying, 'Happy are the dead who die in the faith of Christ! For they shall now rest from their labours, and their good deeds shall follow them to heaven!

or

They shall never feel hunger or thirst, the sun shall not beat on them nor any scorching heat, because the lamb who is at the heart of the throne will be their shepherd and will guide them to the springs of the water of life; and God will wipe all tears from their eyes.

(*The Congregation now seated, the minister will continue:*)
Let us pray:
> O Lord Jesus Christ you are the King of Glory.
> You are the everlasting Son of the Father.
> We therefore pray that you may help your servants
> whom you have redeemed with your precious blood.
> May they be gathered with all your saints
> in everlasting glory.
> This day, Lord, give your servant
> his discharge in peace;
> Now your promise is fulfilled,
> For our eyes have seen your great salvation.

O God whose mercies cannot be numbered, accept our prayers
on behalf of the soul of your servant now departed, and
receive him into the land of light and joy in the fellowship
of all the saints, through Jesus Christ our Lord.

Father in heaven from whom we come and to whom we belong
make us deeply conscious of the shortness and uncertainty of
human life. So may we eagerly grasp the hand of him who will
surely guide us through every perplexing path of life and at
the last, when we have served you in our day and generation,
will bring us to that abode which he promised us in the company
of all your faithful ones, through the same Jesus Christ our
Lord.

O Lord, support us all the day long of this troublous life,
until the shadows lengthen, the evening comes and the busy
world is hushed, the fever of life is over, and our work
done; then Lord in your mercy grant us safe lodging, a holy
rest, and peace at the last, through Jesus Christ our Lord!

Closing Praise

May the peace of God, which is beyond our utmost understanding
and deserving keep guard over your hearts and thoughts, in
Christ Jesus our Lord.   AMEN

SECTION C

New Forms of Worship

1

FAMILY WORSHIP ON THE ·SUNDAY BEFORE CHRISTMAS

'He's only a baby to grow to a man.'

All sing 'Hark! The Herald Angels Sing' (RCH 46).

Then the Minister says:
>The people who walked in darkness
>have seen a great light;
>those who dwelt in a land of deep darkness,
>on them has the light shined.

Let us pray
Father, it is Christmas time, and we are getting ready to enjoy ourselves.
We come now to remember the birth of Jesus, who came that might have life, and that we might have it in all its fullness.
It is only because of Jesus that we know that we can call you 'Father'.
We praise you now for the wonder of your love.
Be with us now as we speak and sing about the joy of Christm.
For Jesus' sake.

AMEN

Sunday School children sing 'The Zither Carol' (*Czech Traditional*)

Then follows this dramatised reading of Luke's account of the nativity (Based on the Jerusalem Bible)

NARRATOR: Caesar Augustus issued a decree for a census of the whole world to be taken. This census took place while Quirinius was governor of Syria; and everyone went to his own town to be registered.

100

JOSEPH: So I, Joseph, set out from the town Nazareth in Galilee, and travelled up to Judaea, to the town of David called Bethlehem, since I am of David's house and line, in order to be registered with Mary, my betrothed, who was with child. While we were there the time came for her to have her child, and she gave birth to a son, her first-born.

MARY: I wrapped him in swaddling clothes, and laid him in a manger, because there was no room for us at the inn.

SHEPHERD: In the countryside close by we shepherds lived in the fields and took it in turns to watch our flocks during the night. The angel of the Lord appeared to us and the glory of the Lord shone round us. We were terrified; but the angel said,

ANGEL: Do not be afraid. Listen, I bring you news of great joy, a joy to be shared by the whole people. Today in the town of David a saviour has been born to you; he is Christ the Lord. And here is a sign for you: you will find a baby wrapped in swaddling clothes and lying in a manger.

NARRATOR: And suddenly with the angel there was a great throng of the heavenly host, praising God and singing:

ANGELS: Glory to God in the highest heaven, and peace to men who enjoy his favour.

SHEPHERD: Now when the angels had gone from us into heaven, we said to each other, 'Let us go to Bethlehem and see this thing that has happened which the Lord has made known to us.' So we hurried away and found Mary and Joseph, and the baby lying in the manger.

MARY: When they saw the child they repeated what they had been told about him, and everyone who heard it was astonished at what the shepherds had to say. As for me, I treasured all these things and pondered them in my heart. And the shepherds went back glorifying and praising God for all they had heard and seen; it was exactly as they had been told.

A soloist sings the first verse and chorus of 'Don't Wait For An Angel' *by Caryl Micklem*

All sing 'Once in Royal David's City' (R.C.H. 69)

1st SPEAKER: Once in royal David's city. What about now in royal David's city?

2nd SPEAKER: What about *all* the cities of today's world?

A soloist sings 'The Present Tense' *by Sydney Carter*

3rd SPEAKER: Bethlehem: Royal David's city is today surrounded by the tragic conflict of Arab and Jew.

4th SPEAKER: Glasgow: Scotland's largest city. The biggest housing problem in the country, but sharing the problem with many cities in affluent Britain.

5th SPEAKER: Johannesburg: A modern cosmopolitan city in country where 11½ million black people are ruled and domina by 3½ million white people.

6th SPEAKER: Saigon: Capital city of South Vietnam, where American soldiers went to defend freedom and found themsel killing old men, and women and children.

2nd SPEAKER: Prague: City with an ancient tradition of freedom, now once again under the heel of an oppressor.

3rd SPEAKER: Lagos: Capital city of a nation torn by the bitterness of tribal warfare.

4th SPEAKER: Athens: Home of democracy, where today a military regime maintains its power by torturing its opponents

5th SPEAKER: Delhi: A city filled with poor and hungry people, reminding us that most of the world's people are hung

6th SPEAKER: Aberdeen: Our city. Our home. The city of our loyalty. Faced, like other cities in our country, with all the problems of a growing and mobile population.

1st SPEAKER: Once in royal David's city is all very well but now in the modern city matters too.

A soloist sings 'Don't Wait For An Angel', *verse 2 and Chorus*

Minister: Let us pray:

Father, once in royal David's city a baby was born.
The baby grew to be a man, and we call ourselves his follower
As his followers, we now pray for the cities of our world,
which are the cities of your world, filled with the people for
whom Jesus lived and died.

Father, give insight and courage to the rulers of the world, so that they may discover what to do, and be able to do it. Fill the hearts of people everywhere with love and compassion — inspire them to find joy in service; so that men and women and children all over the world may love and serve each other in the spirit of Jesus; and so that wherever there is suffering, and wherever there is pain, and wherever there is any kind of trouble or sorrow, your love may transform it, and people may live as you mean them to live. We ask it for Jesus' sake.

AMEN

ALL SING 'Tomorrow Christ is Coming' *by Fred Kaan*

1st SPEAKER: We shall find Christ among us, as child or youth or man.
Where do we see Christ among us today?

2nd SPEAKER: Christian Aid resettles 1,000 refugees a month.

3rd SPEAKER: In three years, SHELTER has raised nearly two million pounds and rehoused 2½ thousand families.

4th SPEAKER: British children who watch the TV programme 'Blue Peter' bought three mobile clinics to help the sick and wounded on both sides in Nigeria-Biafra.

5th SPEAKER: A Scottish missionary in northern India preaches the gospel in words, and demonstrates the gospel in action by helping to dig wells to irrigate the crops.

6th SPEAKER: The people of Czechoslovakia, unable to overthrow their oppressors, continue with courage their passive resistance.

1st SPEAKER: As Catholic and Protestant in Northern Ireland fight in the streets, Belfast shipyard workers of both faiths go on working side by side in peace, and start to build a better relationship.

2nd SPEAKER: At great personal risk, an American soldier in Vietnam removes a live grenade from the face of a Vietcong terrorist.

A soloist sings 'Don't Wait For An Angel', *verse 3 and Chorus*

Minister: Let us pray:
Father, we thank you for all that you have given us.
We thank you for the joy of Christmas, for all the merriment with which we can celebrate the birth of Jesus and all that it means for us.
And we thank you for all that has been done throughout history in the spirit of Jesus, and for every evidence today that men and women and children can carry on the work he began.
We thank you for calling us to play our part in this work, and for giving us the strength to do your will.   AMEN

ALL SING 'Love Came Down At Christmas' (R.C.H. 52)

Sunday School children sing 'The Kings' *by Reginald Barret-Ayres*

3rd SPEAKER: When kings came to visit Jesus, they brought gold, and frankincense and myrrh.

4th SPEAKER: We now bring our gifts, as we make our offering.

The Offering is collected and laid on the table

Minister: Here, Father, we offer some of our money for the work of the Church.
We bring it as a token of our intention to carry on the work that Jesus began.
Accept our offering, Father, for Jesus' sake.

AMEN

5th SPEAKER: The kings brought their gifts, and we have brought ours.
Men in every age have had their own particular gifts to bring.
We have our modern contributions to make.

6th SPEAKER: Now, men can walk on the moon; and men hope to walk on the planets, and travel ever further into space.

Minister: Incredible though it may seem, what happened 'once, in royal David's city' must, if it has any meaning, have meaning there, too.

A folk group sing 'Every Star Shall Sing A Carol' *by Sydney Carter.*

ALL SING 'Child In The Manger' (R.C.H. 53) *while bread and wine are laid on the communion table.*

Minister: Father, every time we bring bread and wine
to be used in this holy fellowship, we offer them to you
as the symbols of what you have given us, and of what we have
done with your gifts.
In this way we offer them now.
In this way we offer ourselves, admitting our sin.
We ask you to transform them and us, so that the bread and
wine may be for us the communion of the body and blood of
Jesus, and so that we may be his body at work in the world.

AMEN

As our Lord Jesus, on the night of his arrest, took bread,
I take this bread and this wine, to be used in this holy
fellowship; and as he gave thanks and blessed, let us again
thank and praise him.

Let us pray.
Blessed be God our Father for the bread of the earth,
    for food and shelter,
    for the toil and skill of man,
    for our common life together,
    for Christ the bread of life.
Blessed be God our Father for the fruit of the vine,
    for the joy and gladness of life,
    for human care and love,
    for the gift and sacrifice of Christ our Lord.[1]
We remember Jesus, who shared our life and our death, and
rose again, bringing us new life.
We pray that as we eat this bread and drink this wine the
Holy Spirit may be with us.
And we join now with Christian people of every age to say

Minister and People:
        Holy, Holy, Holy, mighty Lord God,
        all space and all time show forth your glory;
        we acknowledge it too.
        OUR FATHER......

Minister: We remember now that when Jesus had given thanks, as we have done, he took bread, and broke it, and said, 'Take, eat; this is my body which is for you; do this in remembrance of me.'
And in the same way he took the cup, after supper, and said, 'This cup is the new covenant in my blood; do this, whenever you drink it, in remembrance of me.'

> Jesus lamb of God
> *have mercy on us.*
> Jesus, bearer of the world's sin,
> *have mercy on us.*
> Jesus, redeemer of the world,
> *give us your peace.*[2]

The gifts of God for the people of God.
Take, eat, this is the body of Christ which is for you.
This cup is the new covenant in the blood of Christ, which is shed for many for the remission of sin; drink from it, all of you.

Bread and wine are shared among the communicants.

Minister: Lord, by the love of Christ we are yours –
take us and use us as your people.
The whole earth is yours – here let us work to your glory.

AMEN

ALL SING 'O Come, All Ye Faithful' (R.C.H. 55(i))
Minister: Go, serve the Lord, and rejoice in his love.
And the blessing of God go with you all.
People: AMEN

NOTES
1. Adapted from an order in *Worship for Today*, Epworth Press.
2. From the Church of England Liturgical Commission.

This service was composed in 1969 and certain references are peculiarly topical to that period. Obviously, changes need to be made to give topicality both in time and place.
The words of the songs will be found in the following books:

'Don't Wait for an Angel' in *Faith, Folk and Festivity.*

'The present tense' in *Songs of Sydney Carter, In the Present Tense, 2.*
'Tomorrow Christ is coming' in *Songs for the Seventies (May be sung to the tune Crüger, R.C.H. 154).*
'The Kings' in *New Songs for the Church.*
'Every star shall sing a carol' in *Songs for the Seventies.*

(All the above books are published by Galliard Press, *Songs for the Seventies* jointly with The Saint Andrew Press.)

2
ORDER FOR EVENING SERVICE

People Praying

Guided Meditation and Corporate Silence

'Gloria' (said responsively)

Praise
Reading followed by Prayer and Suggestions.
'Gloria' (said responsively)

Praise

Offering
Prayers of Thanksgiving and Commitment.
'Gloria' (said responsively)

Praise
The Blessing

Purpose
The basic aims of this suggested form of worship are two-fold. First to involve as many people as possible in the total activity of prayer. Second to create a structure within which prayer becomes directly related to people's own experience and is engaged in language meaningful to them.

Plan

We have to recognise that the worshipper arrives in the Church
building as an individual. Even though he may come with his
family, or perhaps sit beside friends, nevertheless to a
large extent he begins sitting by himself as one person.
This means that we have to take into account his individual
thoughts — thoughts and ideas about God, himself, and the
relationship between God and himself. Thus set prayers, whether
they are in ancient or modern English, do not necessarily take
into account the individual's thoughts, nor do they always
express those thoughts in meaningful terms for him. Indeed
set prayers can inhibit and frustrate the individual by
creating images and concepts which may be alien to him. The
only thing we can say about him is that he wants to pray as
he knows how. So we begin the service with the minister
leading 'Guided Meditation and Corporate Silence'.

1. *Guided Meditation and Corporate Silence*
Simply, the minister will invite the people with a variety
of 'bidding sentences' to express and concentrate their
thinking on God, themselves, and the relationship between.
This not only removes the possible inhibitions and frustrations
caused by set prayer, but places the responsibility for praying
fully on the people themselves.
After each 'bidding sentence' there should be a period of
corporate silence to allow the people to pray individually.
But this is also the beginning of the first movement of the
service, namely from individual to corporate, as in the silence
the individuals begin to be drawn together. This first movement of the service ends with an opportunity for the corporate
body to express its re-awakened awareness of its relationship
with God. The 'Gloria' seems to express this best, not just
because of its basic theology, but because of its brevity, its
joy, and perhaps above all, its eternal quality. For at one
and the same time the individuals act corporately in saying
it, and are also united with the whole history of Christian
witness.

2. *Praise*
A Hymn or Psalm of praise or adoration.

3. *Reading/Prayer/Suggestion*
This is the second movement and the central activity of the
service, which is basically one of corporate intercession.
The idea is that, say twice a year, the regular worshipping
congregation should be divided into 'intercessory groups'
each group being given an area of concern to deal with, e.g.
'the parish', 'the Church universal', 'the world and peace',
'industry', etc. The congregation would then allocate particular
groups to particular Sundays, thus making one of them responsible for this part of the service each Sunday
The group would meet with or without the minister towards
the end of the week to discuss their particular area of
concern. They would make themselves fully informed about it,
and being so would then begin to shape their part of the
service.
They would begin with reading from Scripture, newspapers, etc.,
relevant and appropriate to their area of concern, and follow
the readings with prayers of intercession on a responsive
basis. Two or three people would act as spokesmen for the
group, actually doing the reading and leading the prayers.
If the group felt from their meeting that their area of concern also required some practical action, then this action
would be suggested to the congregation. Again this second
movement of the service would end with the 'Gloria', thus
uniting the congregation and allowing those in other groups
to identify themselves with the leading group.
In this the individual, having already been moved into the
corporate, is now further moved into an area of concern which
becomes common to all.

4. *Praise*
A Hymn or Psalm appropriate to the area of concern.

5. *The Offering*
The beginning of the congregation's response to the area of
concern.

6. *Prayers of Thanksgiving and Commitment*

This is the third movement of the service in which first,
all that has gone before is rendered to God in thanksgiving,
and second, the congregation is moved to commit itself to
God and through him to the area of concern
Here the minister, who will lead these prayers, must try to
underline the second movement with theological emphases and
point to the transcendental nature of prayer which gives
the thoughts expressed and the words used a deeper significance.
He must lead the people in a re-dedication to discipleship,
making them aware of the strength which faith provides thereto.
Once more the 'Gloria' acts as the exclamation mark at the
end of these prayers.

7. *Praise*
A Hymn of discipleship or faith and trust.

8. *The Blessing*
The Praying People go out renewed to continue praying.

Summing up
Briefly what has happened. A man has come to worship. His
thoughts have been guided to think of God and his love, and
to think of his own love in return. In doing so he finds
himself united with all the others who have been doing the
same. Together then, all are guided to think of God and his
love for the world, and to think of their love for others.
Finally, grateful for these truths and opportunities, they
dedicate themselves anew, and are blessed as they go back
into the world to continue their witness.

3

A FAMILY SERVICE
(to express a Theology of Worship)

Good Morning! And welcome to this Family Service.
We all belong to some family, some as children, some as
parents, or perhaps as some other relation. And we all have a
family name.
As a congregation too, we have a family name (*The North
and East Church of St Nicholas*) — that is the name of a
kind of family to which we all belong, and you are sitting
now in the family house. Please feel at home.
In this service I want to say some things which we usually
leave unsaid because they are so much part of what we do as
a habit when we are together here. Perhaps we will all —
young and old — find new meaning in what we do together in
church.

We have come to praise God. Let us begin with the hymn of
praise.
(*Hymn, 'All praise to Thee . . .'* (R.C.H. 257). *It ends
'. . . Praise God all creatures here below.'*)

How are we to praise God? Well, I don't think that we can
really do it all on our own — true praise concerns what we
do together. So right at the beginning of our service we say
sorry for what we have done individually and selfishly. It
is our belief that if we are sincere God will forgive us and
that he will help us to try again to be his family. The first
part of our service is always like that — beginning with being
individuals, and moving to become a community, a family again.

So let us pray
Almighty God, King of kings, and Lord of lords, you are the
one behind the whole of our world and the whole of our lives.
You are the one who made it good, and without you and without

111

your continued presence there is disorder and chaos and
trouble.

Lord God, we forget you too easily, we go our own way, we
forget that you depend on people like us if your ways are to
continue to grow and be made known among those whom we me
We forget that if we are part of your family then we have a
part to play or your family is not complete. Lord God, we
are sorry, truly sorry, where we have failed to play our part.
Perhaps we did not do or say the right thing when the opportuni
was present. Perhaps we did things or said things too hastily.
For all the different times when our thought was only for ourselves, when we forgot to consider your way and the needs of
others, we truly repent.

Dear God, our heavenly Father, through Jesus Christ we know
that you forgive, and that you love us. Thank you for the joy
we feel that the past has been forgiven, in as much as we are
sincere. We pray that we might have greater strength in the
future to live as your family, and be less anxious to follow
selfish ways, that we will find in your service the truth
that to serve you completely is to find perfect freedom.

Heavenly Father, we believe that you have restored us to be
together as your family again. And so we can now as one family
all pray saying:
OUR FATHER ......

Let me now tell you the family news. (*The intimations are
given*)

Boys and girls, will you come and help me tell a story.
(*An imaginary story, set in Africa, is told to parallel the
movement of the service thus far. Children in pairs are dotted
over the chancel area. Each pair is visited in turn by a
witch-doctor accompanied by a drummer, and each shows terro
as he comes near. The drum is beaten louder, and a missionary
approaches. He calls all the children together, tells them
of a God who loves them, and wants them to love each other,
so they join hands in a circle. He tells them that God is like
a loving father, and the children dance round, happy, in their
new 'family' circle.*)

112

N.B. No rehearsal is needed and the story with the action
following each part should 'hold' young and old for the
seven minutes it lasts.)

A Children's Hymn

The Junior Choir sings

(*At the Lectern*) In our understanding of what happens
in church we have completed the first movement. This happens
every week — we come as individuals and we become a community
or a family again.

As a family we gather round the Bible because we believe that
through it God speaks to us. So we usually say: let us hear
the Word of God.

The Word

(*At the end of the reading it should be explained that*
the minister usually gives thanks to God for the 'Word', and
commends it to the congregation. Now we would do this as a
family by singing together, 'Lord Thy Word abideth and our
footsteps guideth')

Hymn: 'Lord, Thy word abideth', (R.C.H. 199)

The Sermon
(*This should stress the link with the Word which has just*
been read, that the Sermon is part of the middle movement of
the service, the gathering round the Word as a family, and not
an end in itself. It should also be stated that as a family
we would respond after the Sermon through our offering, our
thanksgiving and our intercessions; further that the Benediction
is not a full-stop but a blessing on our continued response.
The text from Mark 16:8 'They said nothing to anybody . . .' and
the fact that the church has never found the short ending
(i.e. at v 8a) to be complete, allows the above teaching to
be given and the Word preached.)

The Offering

Prayer
Our heavenly Father, thanks be to you for our life and for our
living. Thanks be to you for the joy of being together and of
sharing. Thanks be to you for the memories of others which

we treasure and which direct our path. Thanks be to you for the trust you have placed on us through the responsibilities which are ours, in family, at work, at school, and among our friends. And thanks be to you for our well-being from which we make this offering.

Use the money we bring, the talents we have, to share with the world your Gospel of peace and wholeness. So, we pray, be with the sick, the sad, and the forsaken, and strengthen our family of your church here to serve you where you would serve, and to do what you would do, that we will not in the end be found to respond with silence, saying nothing to anybody (reference to Sermon), but to your name be praise and glory.   AMEN

Hymn

Benediction

        Go on your way in peace, in love, and with joy, and ma
        The grace of the Lord Jesus Christ,
        The love of God our Father,
        And fellowship in His Holy Spirit,
        Be in the lives of each one of us
        Now and always.   AMEN

The General Scheme of the above Service

	Introduction
	Hymn
	Prayer (Adoration, Confession, Acceptanc
The Approach:	Forgiveness, Supplication)
	Intimations
	Children's Action Story and Hymn
	Anthem
	Lesson
The Word:	Hymn
	Sermon
	Offering
	Prayer (Thanksgiving, Dedication,
The Response:	Intercession)
	Hymn
	Benediction

4

MEDITATION ON ASK, SEEK AND KNOCK

Jesus said:
>   Ask and you shall receive;
>   Seek and you shall find;
>   Knock and it shall be opened unto you.

Prayer
O God, you have brought us together in this place today and we
thank you.
We come with many Questions — about the purpose of our
life; about the problems of the world; about the sorrows that
life brings; about the meaning of it all.
We come seeking many things — rest and peace, company and
forgiveness, hope and a new direction to our lives.
We come knocking, because so many doors seemed closed, for
safety or from fear: to keep us out of the unknown.

Lord, we do not ask you to forgive our questions and our
doubts, for you tell us to ask and to seek and to knock.
We ask you to forgive
>   our reluctance to go on asking,
>   our fear of the answers,
>   our unwillingness to open doors which could lead
>   us into a new day.

Lord, your forgiveness of us is made known to us in all that
we receive even before we ask —
>   in beauty, joy and truth freely given to us;
>   in the mercies of our fellow men;
>   in the special gifts of your grace given to each one of us
>   in our family and friends.
Your acceptance of us is made manifest to us
>   in the miracle of our knowing Jesus;

in our finding of him in friend and stranger;
and in all the common mysteries of daily life.
Your call to us is heard
in the doors that are open to us in the world today;
in the fact of a world made one in economic inter-
dependence;
in the possibility of the conquest of hunger, disease
and ignorance;
and in our desperate hope of peace.
Thanks be to you for the call to ask and seek and knock which
comes to us from Jesus.

'God, who commanded the light to shine out of darkness, hath
shined in in our hearts, to give the light of the knowledge of
the glory of God in the face of Jesus Christ.' (2 Corinthians
4:6)

Prayer
O God, it is your light that shines on the world — to reveal
its truth and to help us to live. We thank you for the light
of the world: that it makes us see not only what we want to
see but what we ought to see; that it reveals the wonder of
the world, its beauty, its mystery and its pain. We thank you
that it shows us ourselves as part of the world; our achievements and our failures.

We pray for all who suffer deeply from what they
have seen in your world, especially for those who
mourn the loss of those they love, for those who
suffer from the cruelty of their fellow-men, for
those who have seen their hopes destroyed.
These your children, for whom the world has become
a lonely place,
Uphold in your love

We pray for those who seek to understand the secrets
of the universe, that they may find them to be the
secrets of your kingdom; for scientists, artists,
politicians.

These your children, in their questioning, their
patience and their faith
    Uphold in your love.

O God, it is your light that shines in our hearts — to lead
us out into the world, to bring us into life with others, to
find the glory of our life in your love. We thank you that
we can love and suffer, be angry and have hope. We thank you
that you have made us in your own image.
    We pray for men and women in their homes and in their
    daily work, bound in affection to their families,
    bound in necessity to the service of their fellows
    in their daily work.
These your children in their service of their
neighbours
    Uphold in your love.

We pray for those who seek to break down the barriers
we erect to make our lives comfortable and to save
us from caring — those who care for the refugee and
the prisoner, those who work against racial dis-
crimination, injustice and war. These your children,
whoever they may be, in their efforts to love their
neighbours
    Uphold in your love.

O God , by your light in the world and by your light in our
hearts, you have made us to know its glory in the face of
Jesus Christ. We thank you for your Church and for our place
in it. We thank you for the light that is ours in the company
of Jesus and of all who share his light.
We pray for your Church throughout the whole world; that its
members everywhere may walk in that light and may help the
world to know its true light.
All your children everywhere, in their joyful acceptance of
your light
    Uphold in your love.

OUR FATHER . . . . . .

5

MORNING PRAYERS AT IONA ABBEY

Leader — Awaken us, Lord.
ALL — *Awaken us to a sense of your presence*
Leader — Lord, we have faith
ALL — *Help us in doubt and uncertainty*
Leader — Your love goes before us
ALL — *Help us to follow with joy*
A Hymn of Praise
Prayer (*Begins with extempore prayer after which the leader
will say:* 'Let us admit our need')
WE ADMIT OUR NEED
ALL Lord we admit that our faith is weak, our love is cold
and our hope is dying.
We have locked ourselves within our own small worlds.
We are afraid to open our lives to you and to others.
Help us to make a fresh start and to go forward together
with you.

WE DECLARE OUR FAITH
Leader
Lord Jesus, when you lived amon us, you gave us a living faith.
When you died on the cross, you gave us a love that pushes us
outside ourselves.
When you came back from death, you gave us new hope.
Because you are with us, we can be fully ourselves.

WE RECOMMIT OURSELVES
ALL Lord God, we offer ourselves again to you today, asking
that you will show us what we need to do.
We offer ourselves again to one another, asking that we
may grow together in love.
Through Jesus Christ our Lord,   AMEN

Lesson for the Day

Hymn of Dedication

Prayer of intercession

(Will include prayers for members of the Iona Community by name. The prayer — and the service — will end with the congregation saying together the following version of the Lord's Prayer.)

Our Heavenly Father,

May your name be honoured.

May your Kingdom come, and your will be done on earth as it is in heaven.

Give us this day the bread we need.

Forgive us what we owe to you, as we have also forgiven those who owe anything to us.

Keep us clear of temptation, and save us from evil.

For the kingdom and the power and the glory are yours for ever.   AMEN

6

SERVICES ON SPECIAL THEMES

THE INDIVIDUAL

(I)

Jesus said, 'If one of you has a hundred sheep and loses one, does he not go after the missing one until he has found it?'

'The Lord is my shepherd.'

>Lord God, Creator of men, we give you our worship.
>Lord God, Saviour of men, we give you our worship.
>Lord God, Renewer of men, we give you our worship.

119

As we marvel at what great things you have done, help us to take in the scope of your love — a love that is for all of us, but also for each of us — a love which can make new men and women of us.

Some of us need shepherding and leading.
Some of us feel lost . . . some of us are lost . . . we call for help . . . we long to be found.
Some of us feel unimportant, swept aside by the pressures of life, as if we do not count, do not matter to anyone.

Lord, be our shepherd — convince us that we are looked after, and led, and restored, and accompanied, in life and death.

May we go from here today to life as it awaits us, saying in our hearts, 'The Lord is my shepherd . . . The Lord is my shepherd . . .'

And in words of Jesus we pray together,
OUR FATHER . . . . . .

(II)
For all we owe to you, Lord God, we are grateful,
for new insight into the gospel, new encouragement to face life, new sympathy for other people, new ideas for being of service to them

for those who have made us what we are — parents, husband and wife, wise friends — people to whom we belong and are important — people who give us the courage and the energy to live

for Jesus — for all he has made possible, for his gentleness and courtesy, for all he means to us.

So we pray for others . . . . . .
Today we pray for people whose lives have been overwhelmed by forces far beyond their control, people who feel helpless, unheard, unnoticed, insignificant, doomed.

We think of the people of . . . . . ., caught in the crossfire of civil war, — of refugees, of hostages, — wondering what will become of them.

     Lord, listen to their cry — and to our cry for them . . .

120

We think of people trying to protest against injustice and
evil, yet feeling powerless to gain a hearing, or to make any
impression, or bring about any change.

We think of prisoners, guilty only of challenging iniquity,
of exiles, of those who are being persecuted for their beliefs
and their convictions.
> Lord, listen to their cry — and to our cry for them . . .

We think of people who in spite of the sympathy and help of
others still feel isolated and forsaken.
We think of people who are ill, physically or mentally — of
old people, baffled by the pace of this age — of young people,
feeling misunderstood and resented.
> Lord, listen to their cry — and to our cry for them . . .

We think, in silence, of any person, any problem, that we
want to commit to God here and now . . .
> Lord, listen to their cry — and to our cry for them . . .

And join our prayers and our lives and our witness to that of
the Christian saints who have gone before us, and who wait
for us in the presence of your glory, full of joy. From them
and us, receive all praise and blessing, now and for evermore.

*   *   *

DISABILITY
(I)
'To shame what is wrong, God has chosen what the world counts
weakness — so there is no place for human pride in the presence
of God.'

Scarcely can we find words, Lord God, to express how we
honour and worship and love you — for taking people like
us, and bringing us together, and calling us the Church, the
body of Christ — with all our incompetence, our inadequacy,
our timorous caution, our lack of faith — for taking such
as us, to carry your strength and your power into the world
and into the lives of others.

121

We are proud, but not of ourselves — we are proud of our
Lord, and of what he can do.

Deal with us, Lord, so that we can be of more use to you.
If we feel sorry for ourselves . . .
If we see only our problems, and not our potential . . .
If we are merely frustrated at what we cannot do, and not
excited about what we can do . . .
If we are touchy and oversensitive . . .
— then deal with us, Lord, and make new men and women of us.

Jesus said, 'I came to call not the virtuous, but sinners,
to change their ways.'

So call us, do something with us, make something of us, use
our very weakness of mind, spirit, body, to show more
plainly your strength and your glory.

*   *   *

(II)
Let us with new understanding praise God.
Lord God, we offer thanks, humbly, for giving us life, and
for all the challenges of life that have brought out the
best in us.
We offer thanks for what we do have, and can do, for skills
that we might never have learned, friends we might never
have met, insights we might never have seen, had life been
easy and free of all pain and set-back.
We offer thanks for the patience with which you bear with
us, and forgive and renew us again and again, pick us up
when we fall — and for the quietness and calm that still
waits for us after our storms of anger and frustration.
We offer thanks for Jesus, who loved life, and faced life
at its worst — who went through hell, to blaze a trail for
us in whose living and present strength we too can live
triumphantly.
Lord God, we offer thanks . . .

And let us with new insight pray for others—
for people we have spoken of this morning, people who can-

not move about, cannot hear, or see, or speak easily . . .

for people whose scars are in the mind and the heart, who hate life, and hate themselves, who fear even gentleness when it is offered them . . .

for people bowed down with a burden of guilt, of something they have never owned up to, or of something they are now paying the penalty for . . .

for people who find day-to-day living difficult, because of its decisions, its responsibilities, its demands on them . . .

for people who cannot get through to God, though they long to share the faith they see in others . . .

for those who make it their business to try and help, to heal, console, encourage, advise, befriend, to love their neighbour as Jesus taught . . .

and for our best-beloved — our families, husband, wife, parents, children, brother, sister, life-long friend — those who have given us so much, and in giving have taught us how to give in return . . .

O God, the Father of all, give to those we now remember great courage and persistence to overcome the difficulties that can be overcome, and grace to accept the limits that cannot be crossed. And to all of us give something of the active, energetic love of Jesus, that we may truly be members of his body, truly children of the one family of the Father, who with the Christ and the Spirit lives and reigns for ever.

7

AN ORDER OF SERVICE FOR A SMALL COMMUNION

Note

This order is designed for use in circumstances where a small group of people who know each other are meeting round a table. The Upper Room atmosphere is the aim, rather than the 'churchy'.

The leader should make sure that the narrative quality is maintained, giving out the 'parts' well beforehand.

If there is time, and if there are enough articulate people involved, more passages from the Last Supper narrative could be included. Where a group meets for communion frequently, there is enough material in the gospels to provide for different passages to be read on different occasions. But even using these passages each time, while giving them to different members of the group, it will be found that there is an interesting variety.

The order is as follows:

Laying the table

Invocation

Reading: John 13 (*The Washing of the feet*)
    followed by prayer of confession.

Reading: John 14 (*The Way . . .*)
    followed by prayer about the future, the Way ahead.

Reading: John 15 (*The Vine*)
    followed by prayer for one another, and for the
    Church.

Reading: I Cor. 11 (*The Institution*)

The Act of Communion.

Thanksgiving.

(In the above order, no indications of verses are given. Obviously the whole chapter would be too long, but the reader has some latitude in which section he uses.)

FOR A SMALL COMMUNION

The leader opens the service saying words such as:
'We remember how Jesus sent Peter and John, saying:
> Go and make ready the Passover for us, that we may
> eat. With desire have I desired to eat this Passover
> with you before I suffer.'

LAYING THE TABLE

In the name of Jesus,
> we now lay the table, that he may eat with us.

This bread and wine, and all the preparations we have made,
> we now offer to our Lord:

We, his disciples, having done as we were told,
> await his coming to take his place in our midst:

Let us pray
Jesus, Lord,
The table is ready,
> We, your disciples await your presence.

Bread and wine cannot nourish our souls,
Our fellowship will soon break up,
And each one of us would soon revert to type, unless you
come and fill all things with your presence.

In your presence,
Bread and wine are alive with the life that makes all things
new.
Our fellowship becomes the body of Christ,
And each one of us is lifted up to a new level.

INVOCATION

Come, Lord Jesus,
> take your rightful place as host at this your table.

Come, Lord Jesus,
> take your rightful place as Lord of your Church.

Come, Lord Jesus,
> take your rightful place as King of our lives.
> Come, Lord Jesus, come.

(Silence)
'Behold I stand at the door and knock,
if any man hear my voice and open the door

I will come in and sup with him, and he with me.'

Glory be to the living Christ who comes to us,

Glory be to the living Christ, mighty in the battle against
   the powers of darkness.

Glory be to the living Christ, who comes to save us.

Psalm 24:7 can be sung here

THE WASHING OF THE FEET

Reading from John 13.

(The idea is that the person reading it should follow on with
some thoughts on how this ties up with the life of the group,
and what it has been discussing.

A prayer should arise out of this.

In the event of difficulty over this, Psalm 51 could be read
responsively.)

*The prayer may be summed up in the words of the mutual
confession:*

> I confess to God almighty, in the sight of the
> whole company of heaven, and before you all, that
> I have sinned exceedingly in thought, word and deed,
> through my fault, my own fault, my own most grievous
> fault, wherefore I pray God almighty to have mercy
> upon me.
>
> *May the almighty and merciful Lord grant you pardon,*
> *absolution, and remission of your sins, time for*
> *amendment of life, and the comfort of his Holy*
> *Spirit.   AMEN*

(*The above to be repeated, the responder taking the
versicle*)

O Jesus

> We thank you for your patience with us, your disciples.
> We thank you that we can make a clean start once more.
> We thank you for not holding our sins against us.

Here and now we pray for those with whom we have quarrelled,
   those who have wronged us,
      those whom we have wronged.

We forgive them, even as you have forgiven us.

And if there are hidden tensions below the surface of our
    fellowship as we gather round your table,
      enable us to face them and set them right, for your own
    Name's sake we ask it.   AMEN

THE WAY

Reading from John 14.
(The person taking this section should bring into focus
one or two of the things about the future that worry this
particular group of people.
A prayer should follow, laying it all before the Lord.
In the event of difficulty, here is a pattern-prayer. It is
not meant to be used word for word, but as a general lead.)

Jesus,
    we will not be troubled or afraid as we face the
    future.
    We do not know what lies ahead,
    but we know you, and that is enough.
    So in quiet confidence we lay before you these
    things that concern us . . .

Jesus, the Way, the Truth and the Life,
    You are the Way for us,
      even when we cannot see the next step ahead.
    You are the Truth for us,
      even when the familiar landmarks of life disappear.
    You are the Life for us,
      even when these mortal bodies crumble to dust.
Jesus, the way, the truth and the life,
    armed with your peace,
    we face the future,
    sure that you will lead us safely home,
    in spite of our tendency to wander.
Jesus, the way, the truth and the life,
    in you we put our trust,
    we will trust and not be afraid,
    because you live we shall live also,
    in time and in eternity.   AMEN

The Creed, or some other affirmation of faith may be said here

THE LIVING VINE

Reading from John 15. (The J. B. Phillips version of this is very suitable for a group reading. It stresses the relationship of the branches to each other.)

(Here is the place to consider the real needs of the group, spiritual, financial, health and so on. No particular words are needed, just speaking the names of the people present, leaving a silence after the name. Presumably the group know each other well enough to have some idea of the needs of the person named, and if not, the preliminary conversation should have been a preparation for this.
This should lead into a prayer for the wider church, although, perhaps, it might be worth taking another section of John 17, if one has the time and the people.
No words are really needed to express 'love for one another', but in case it is felt that some are needed, some thoughts are given.)

Lord we thank you for linking us together
    as branches in one great net-work . . . the living vine.
We thank you for our common concerns,
    and for the knowledge that you are working through us.
We thank you for the help we are able to give each other,
    and for the love of Christ at work in our midst.
We thank you for the wide outspread of this vine,
    the network of branches spreading out into every corner
    of the earth,
        spreading beyond earth, into heaven itself.
And now, linked together in the love of Christ,
sharing in the life of the vine,
united with the Church on earth and in heaven we pray:
OUR FATHER . . . . . .

THE INSTITUTION

The words of Institution in I Corinthians 11:23-26.
(Alternatively the version in Mark 14:22-23 may be used.)

In the name of Jesus we do this,
doing what he did, so that we may know him present in our midst.
I now take bread and wine, as he did,
the fruit of God's good earth,
the products of the labour of our brothers and sisters.
They are your gifts, Lord,
and we offer them to you, so that you may use them.
As Jesus gave thanks that night,
so let us thank God now:

To you, O God, we lift up our hearts in thanksgiving,
For you have made us for yourself,
In you we live and move and have our being,
By your love in Jesus Christ you have rescued us,
By your Spirit you renew us daily.

To you then we turn in joy and in love,
united here at your table with all your family,
those on earth and those in heaven,
and in that wonderful unity which you give us
we join in the eternal hymn:
> *Holy, holy, holy, Lord God of Hosts,*
> *Heaven and earth are full of your glory,*
> *Glory be to you, O Lord most high.*

Send down on us, and on these your gifts of bread and wine,
your Holy Spirit,
So that the bread we break and share may be for us
communion in the body of Christ,
and the cup we share may truly be for us
communion in the life-blood of Christ.
So may Christ live in us and we in him.
Here, once again we offer ourselves to you, body and soul,
to be your people, united in your love,
equipped by your Spirit to carry out the work of Christ.
And as your people we are joined together
through Jesus Christ our Lord.

THE DISTRIBUTION

Jesus took bread, broke it and gave it to them saying,
> 'This is my body. It is broken for you.'

(*Bread is broken and passed round the table, each eating his piece*)

And he took the cup saying,
>'This cup is the new covenant. It is sealed in my
>blood.'
>Drink from it, all of you.

(*The cup is passed round, or, if there are separate glasses, the bottle or decanter is passed round, each pouring out his neighbour's glass. If there are separate glasses, then the 'family' can wait till all are served before eating and drinking. If there is one cup, then, obviously each drinks in turn.*)

The peace of the Lord Jesus Christ be upon you all.

THANKSGIVING

O God Our Father,
>We thank you for giving us these tangible tokens of
>your love.
>We thank you for giving us these visible signs of
>our forgiveness.
>We thank you for giving us this real pledge of our
>one-ness,
>>our one-ness with you,
>>and our one-ness with each other.

With new courage we set out to face life,
>trusting in the inner reinforcement that Christ gives us.
With the new light you have given us,
>we tackle the problems which once seemed too great for u
With the love of Christ in our hearts,
>we set out to serve the people we meet on life's journey.

We pray for those whom we shall meet:
>at home . . .
>at work . . .
>in our neighbourhood . . .
We think of those who suffer, especially any we know . . .
May the reality of the presence of Christ in our lives bring
to each of these a blessing.

Father, into your hands we commit ourselves
   and all our loved ones wherever they may be,
   on earth or in heaven.
Glory be to God our Father who loves us.
Glory be to Christ, our living Lord and our Redeemer,
Glory be to the Holy Spirit, powerfully active in our hearts,
To Father, Son and Holy Spirit be praise and glory for ever.
                          AMEN

An Alternative Form for a Fellowship Meal
(If there is no minister, if some members of the group are
not communicants, or belong to denominations which would
object to their members taking part in a sacrament, the
alternative form avoids the words of consecration and institu-
tion, and provides for a fellowship meal which is not, strictly
speaking, a sacrament.)

Reading from John 17.

Comment: St John has told us much about what Jesus did and
         said at the Last Supper, but he says nothing about
         bread and wine, even though the other gospels make
         it central. Instead, he leaves us with our Lord's
         prayer that we should be one, and sharing bread and
         wine is a sign of one-ness, communion. As St Paul
         points out:
         Because there is one loaf, we, many as we are, are
         one body, for it is one loaf of which we all partake.

In the name of the Lord Jesus I now offer you this
bread and wine as the pledges of his love for
you:
The love that suffers over your sins on the Cross,
The love that gives you life which conquers death,
The love which enables you to carry on his work.

In the name of the Lord Jesus I invite you to share
this bread and wine as tokens
      that you accept his love into your life
      that you accept one another as brothers and
      sisters,

that you accept his call to serve him here
on earth.

Sharing Let us now share this loaf in his name.
(*It is passed round, each taking a slice and
passing it on*)
I will take the cup of salvation and call on the
name of the Lord.
(*The bottle is passed, each pouring his neigh-
bour's glass.*)
Let us eat and drink to the glory of God.
(*The bread and wine are eaten in silence*)

The Peace The peace of the Lord Jesus be with us all.

8

A DANCE DRAMA ON THE WORK OF THE HOLY SPIRIT—EVENING SERVICE FOR THE DAY OF PENTECOST

Hymn: 'Jesus stand among us' (R.C.H. 248)
Call to prayer
Take courage, all you people of the land, says the Lord;
work, for I am with you, according to the promise that I mac
you . . . my Spirit abides among you; fear not.
Prayer
O God, the Holy Spirit, come to us, and among us:
come as the wind, and stir us to new life;
come as the fire, and burn away all that is impure;
come as the dew, and give us the sparkling freshness
of dawn.

132

Convict, convert, and consecrate our hearts and lives, making
us whole and holy, to our great good and your greater glory;
   And this we ask for Jesus Christ's sake.

In expressing our Christian faith we use different words to
refer to the one God; and, in particular, the words 'Father',
'Son', and 'Holy Spirit'.
Today, on the Day of Pentecost, the Church celebrates the
descent of the Holy Spirit, the coming of God's power to
give life to the Church, as it is recorded in the second
chapter of the Book of Acts. From that time, the work of the
Spirit was clearer, more sharply defined, than before, but it
was not an entirely new work. In this act of worship we
celebrate the work of the Spirit from the beginning.

Dr William Barclay writes: 'It is the Spirit of God who brings
existence out of nothingness, order out of chaos, beauty out
of blank formlessness. All the thinkers of the ancient times were
impressed with the mystery of the dependableness of this
world. What is it that ceaselessly maintains the rhythm of
night and day, of spring, summer, autumn, and winter, of the
ebb and flow of the tides, and the rising and setting of the
sun? . . . What is it that makes cause and effect predictable?
. . . What is it that makes this a reliable universe in which
we can have faith? . . . The answer of the Old Testament
thinker would be that the Spirit of God brought order into
chaos, and maintains the order of the world . . . If we wish to
see the work of the Spirit, we have no further to look than
at the wonderful world in which we live, for that world is
ordered by the Spirit of God.'

The opening of the Book of Genesis meditates on the coming of
order to the primitive chaos:

(*1st sequence, with reading of Genesis 1:1-5 and 2:7*)

Hymn:'Come, Holy Ghost, our hearts inspire' (R.C.H. 196)

Of all the features of Israel's faith, that which perhaps
contributes most to its unique character is *prophecy* —
not the long-range forecasting of future events, but insight

133

into the consequences of present happenings and the declaration of the will of God. No prophet would have claimed that this was a merely human ability: it was, as the hymn suggested the work of the Spirit in him. An unnamed prophet whose prophecies are incorporated with those of Isaiah, says of himself:

(*2nd sequence with reading of Isaiah 61:1-3*)

Yet the activity of the Spirit of God was not confined to a few select individuals. The Spirit was active in the whole of Israel, and when Israel, in exile in Babylon, was beginning to lose heart and to lose hope, the prophet Ezekiel spoke to them of the power of the Spirit to give new life to the people:

(*3rd sequence, with reading of Ezekiel 37: 1-14*)

It was part of the belief of the Jewish people that in every conception and birth, three parties were active, the two parents, and also the Spirit of God. The story of the birth of our Lord suggests that through the faith of Mary the Spirit was present to a unique degree:

(*4th sequence, with reading of Luke 1:30-35*)

The Magnificat, read responsively. (R.C.H. 715)

What was true of the birth of Jesus was true also of his life. He was the man who was completely open to the guiding and leading of the Spirit of God:

(*5th sequence, with reading of Mark 1:9-12*)

The whole of the life of Jesus, healing the sick, and teaching with authority and 'not as the scribes', was a demonstration of the power of the Spirit. Jesus assured his followers that this same power would be available to them. The story of the Day of Pentecost is the story of their awareness of the coming of that power:

(*6th sequence, with reading of Acts 2:1-4, 12-21*)

Hymn:'Gracious Spirit, Holy Ghost' (R.C.H. 484)

It would be a tragic mistake to suppose that the work of the Spirit ended when the latest book of the Bible had been

written. The results of his activity are to be seen in all
Christian lives. Paul tells us what these results, the
harvest of the Spirit, are; but we make no attempt to portray
them for you. It is the role of each one of us to act out
these things in our daily lives:
(*reading of Galatians 5:16-25*)

Prayer
Trusting in this, your Word, O Lord, we again pray for the
coming of your Spirit. Send him to us to penetrate the deep
places of our lives which without him are dark and formless.
Give us grace to remain humble and still under his action,
that he may comfort our hearts and establish us in his
strength. Bring our conflicting wills to agreement in your
will, and knit us together in one fellowship in the Spirit.
Baptize your whole Church with fire, that her divisions may
soon be overcome, and that she may stand before the world as
a pillar and buttress of your truth. May the Holy Spirit
speak by the voice of your servants in every place who preach
your Word.
Send the Holy Spirit as Comforter to all who face adversity,
or who are victims of men's wickedness. Preserve all nations
and their leaders from hatred and war, and build up a true
community, among nations, through the power of your Spirit;
through Jesus Christ our Lord, in whose prevailing words we
pray, saying:
OUR FATHER......

Hymn: 'Holy Spirit, Truth Divine' (R.C.H. 193)

Benediction

A note on Dance-Drama
Each of the passages of Scripture was interpreted by a group
of girls making interpretative movements — somewhat difficult
to explain. The point is to try to get them to express
through their movements the 'feel' of the passage for them.
Music from records was also used at certain points.

In situations where it would be difficult or undesirable to
interpret the scripture readings in dance movements the material

could be used with some additional hymns or anthems as a service of lessons and praise. The following are suggested as possible items for inclusion:

In connection with the first sequence, 'Creator Spirit! by whose aid' and 'Spirit of God that moved of old' (*R.C.H. 184 and 185*)
In connection with the third sequence, 'Breathe on me, Breath of God' (*R.C.H. 194*)
In connection with the fourth sequence. 'Angelus ad Virginem' (*Oxford Book of Carols 52*)
In connection with the fifth sequence, 'Spirit of God, descend upon my heart' (*R.C.H. 195*)
In connection with the sixth sequence 'All people at this hour' (*Oxford Easy Anthem Book 20*)

Also suitable are 'O Spirit of the living God' (*R.C.H. 386*), 'Spirit of mercy, truth and love' (*to be included in the new Hymn Book*), 'Come Holy Ghost, our souls inspire' (*R.C.H. 182 and Church Anthem Book 13*), 'Come O Creator Spirit come' (*Church Anthem Book 14*)

SECTION D

The Christian Year and Occasional Services

1

FOUR PRAYERS FOR ADVENT

I. 'Jesus — Immanuel'

Lord God, Immanuel — king of kings, yet housed in the meanest
of dwellings — we bless you for still coming to us, for being
with us, for leading us on to a new creation which shall
have a place for all, and where all will be at home.

We are grateful for what you give and what you do;
> for our homes, and what they mean to us . . .
> for so quickening the conscience of man that we
> refuse to be content with low standards . . .
> for people and organisations who have taken the
> initiative, and brought hope to the desperate.

We praise you, Lord, for all the signs that you are truly
Immanuel — God with us.

So we are impelled to pray for others and with others who
long to see justice and beauty and security and peace.

We pray for those who do not have a home of their own;
> young parents searching for a room,
> children and parents separated from each other;

And we pray with those who work with such families to find
room for them in life;
> for Shelter, and all its supporters, young and old;
> for social workers and doctors, who try to support
> people in such troubles;
> for authorities and councillors and officials, whose
> awesome task it is to make houses enough for all.

We pray for all the needy and unwanted of our world;
> all who meet closed doors, closed hearts;
> all who have failed to compete for the money, the
> power, and the places in the world;

137

And we pray with those who refuse to let this be, who work for a better world, who try to be good neighbours, with an open door and an open heart, with sympathy and tolerance.

So we pray, Lord, confident in your power, your kingdom, your glory, for ever.

II. 'Jesus — Son of David'

Lord God, we praise you for those who prepared the way for the Saviour to come
>   for the people of Israel, their prophets, and their
>   kings, struggling to grasp the marvels of your
>   ways, until they became a cradle for the Messiah.

And we pray for Jewish people today,
>   for the state of Israel, the centre of so much
>   striving and struggling and tension;
>   for Jewish people who have made their home here;
>   for Jews still unable to accept Jesus as their
>   Messiah, still waiting and hoping.

We praise you for the security and orderly government by which we live, grateful for all who serve us in politics, in national and local government.

And we pray for our Queen and the members of the Royal family, for Members of Parliament and those who represent us there, for the Lord Provost, Magistrates, Councillors and officials of this city.

We praise you for our freedom to think, speak, worship as we please — for those in past days who gained this freedom for us, who framed our laws, built our schools and churches, laid the foundations of our way of life.

And we pray for people who live under oppressive and tyrannical regimes, to whom freedom and dignity are but dreams — people who are looked down upon, degraded and dispossessed, because they are different in belief, in custom, in colour.

We praise you for our own families, and especially for our forebears, for those whose gifts and strengths have been handed down to us.

And we pray for anyone in our family circle who specially

needs to be strong and to be encouraged just now, as they face a crisis in their lives.

We give our praise and we make our prayers through Jesus Christ, our King and Lord, to whom be glory for ever.

III. 'Jesus — Son of Mary'

We marvel and we rejoice, O God, that for all your splendour and might and freedom you came to us so quietly, so humbly, so helplessly. You asked no privileges, claimed no status. You entered human life as we do, as one of a family, as a baby to be cherished and guarded, loved and tended.

So we can understand better, and see our part more plainly, and we thank you, because of Jesus, Son of Mary.

And seeing this, we can see better how to pray
> for families and homes, for our neighbours and our friends;

> for young couples getting married, creating their home with pride and delight;

> for those expecting a baby, their first-born maybe, preparing to welcome their child, and to lavish their love and care;

> for mothers bearing a child, with no husband to be father, anxious and hurt, wondering what to do for the best;

> for families facing problems — not enough money, not enough food, not enough space, no home at all;

> for families with all that money can buy, yet divided and unhappy, misunderstanding one another;

> for families where the breadwinner is on strike, tense, bleak and defiant;

> for people who don't live in families, but alone, missing the sound of young voices or responsibility for someone other than themselves;

> and for our own family, as we know it, as you know it, Lord . . .

These are our prayers. In your ingenuity, find a use for them,
and a use for us, to bring love for others, and to bring still
more praise to you, our heavenly father, through Jesus Christ.

IV. 'Jesus – Saviour'

Jesus, Immanuel, God with us
be with people in their loneliness, the loneliness of pain,
of grief, of unpopularity, of imprisonment . . .

Jesus, Son of David
be strength and guidance to those who bear authority and
govern peoples, to our Queen and those who rule under her.
Restrain those who rule their peoples with tyranny and
oppression, and give hope to those who long to see right
prevail in their land.

Jesus, Son of Mary
be with people in their families and their homes in this
season, to draw them closer together. Be with little children,
in their excitement and their wonder. Be with any whom
Christmas, with its warmth and its love, will pass by.

Jesus, Saviour
come to the rescue of the sinner, the outcast, the forsaken.
Come wherever friends cannot be found, where tears blind the
eyes, when darkness falls, and pain is all around. Come, and
be a bridge over all the troubled waters of our living.

Jesus, the beginning and the ending, the same yesterday, today
and for ever, we remember with happiness and pride the
Christians of past days, who served you well – the strong
people who left something of their strength to us. As we
wait for the end and the fulfilment of all things, encourage
us by the thought of them, and by the vision of your kingdom.

Glory be to the Father, and to the Son, and to the Holy
Spirit, as it was in the beginning, is now, and shall be
evermore, world without end.

2

THE SECOND SUNDAY IN ADVENT (BIBLE SUNDAY)

I.

Lord God, Creator and Saviour: with all the heavenly company
and with all your people in this world we adore you.
Heaven and earth spell out your splendour.
In Jesus Christ you manifest your love.
With wonder and thanksgiving we acclaim you.

Lord, before you we bow in penitence.
> You have the right to rule in us, but time and again
> we reject you.
> Your Word we have despised.
> Your Spirit we have spurned.
> Your love we disbelieve.
> Your promises we doubt.
> Lord, pity our weakness.
> Forgive us our frailty and folly.
> In Christ's name we ask.

Lord Jesus, John your apostle wrote: 'If we confess our sins,
he is just, and may be trusted to forgive our sins and cleanse
us from every kind of wrong.'

Our sins we have confessed. Give us now the assurance of your
forgiveness and the power of your cleansing from wrong.

Lord God, whose word and will are made known in Jesus Christ:
inspire in us faith in that word and obedience to that will,
for our salvation and for your glory.

Christ Jesus, make us truly your people.
> Let us be gentle and never harsh.
> Let us be patient and never overbearing.
> Let us be compassionate and never hurtful.
> Let us be forgiving and never vindictive.
> Let the love men saw in you also be seen in us.

God, who gave us the Bible to be a lamp to our feet, a light
to our path: by your Holy Spirit open it to our understanding,
that by it we may grow in faith and obedience; through Jesus
Christ our Lord, to whom with you and the Spirit, be glory,
always.

II.
Lord God, King of all creation: we give you thanks for all
your goodness day by day.
Above all, we thank you for Jesus Christ your own true Son,
who took our nature upon him, and died and was raised for our
salvation.

Especially this day we thank you for the Bible, for the insight,
joy, and comfort it brings to believing hearts.
We thank you for Bible translators and publishers, and for
the Church's scholars and teachers who have opened up the
Bible to our understanding.
Grant us, Lord, always to live to your praise; through Christ
our Saviour.

Hear us, Father Almighty, as we intercede in the name of him
who intercedes for us, our Saviour Jesus Christ.
For the Church in all the world, that it may be strong in
faith, ardent in witness, and unwearied in service;

For the Church of Scotland, that it may always proclaim your
Word to our people with patience, zeal, and devotion;
For the missionaries of our Church overseas, that they may be
guided, strengthened, and inspired in every task;
For the National Bible Society of Scotland, that its work may
grow and flourish to the saving nurture of many souls;

For the nations, that unity and peace may be their prime aims,
and that brotherhood may grow between peoples of diverse race
and colour;
For the United Nations Organization, that its influence may
expand to achieve better relations between states;

For every place where there is tension or strife, that forbearance and the will to peace may burgeon;

For the Queen, the Prime Minister, the members of the Cabinet,
and all in Parliament, that they may always be guided to wise
and fruitful decisions;
For those who manage our industry and commerce and those who
lead our trade unions, that they may work harmoniously for
the economic well-being of the nation;
For all in trouble of body, mind, or spirit, especially those
known to us, that they may be healed and comforted, each
according to his need;
Lord, hear our prayer; and let our cry for help reach you.

Eternal God, whose mercy endures for ever: we give thanks for
all who have died in the faith of Christ, especially those
dear to us, . . . Grant us so to be faithful throughout our
earthly pilgrimage, that with them we may share in the glories
of the world to come; through Jesus Christ our Lord, who
lives and reigns with you, Father, and the Holy Spirit, one
God, evermore.

3

A CHRISTMAS EVE SERVICE

(*At about 11 p.m. carol singing, led by somebody
who will not be taking part in the service itself, provides
the gathering point, so that people can drift in, and find a
warm, informal atmosphere. This is important, for many who
come are not used to churches.*)
At 11.30 the minister and helpers enter

Hymn: 'Hark the Herald Angels sing' (R.C.H. 46)

Prayer of Approach
'Come, let us go to Bethlehem,
to see for ourselves this thing that has happened.'

Let us pray
O God, we turn once more towards Bethlehem,
> Help us to find Christ for ourselves.
Through the darkness of doubt
> we stumble to find the Way.
Through the fogs created by our own selfishness and greed,
> we grope for the Truth.
Through the forests of superstition and commercialism that
have grown up around Christmas,
> we struggle to find the secret of Life.

Merciful God, may we not go from here without having received
a blessing, don't allow us to waste another Christmas, seeing
only our own greed.
Help us not to miss the point again.

Grant us light to see where we have gone wrong,
> courage to face our own faults,
> and love strong enough to set things right.
So may this service mark a new beginning for us,
> may something of Christ be born in US tonight,
> making us truly brothers and sister in one great
> family.
This we dare to ask because of the Love you have shown us in
Jesus Christ Our Lord,   AMEN

Reading: Luke 2:1-7
And we continue the story in singing the Hymn . . .

Hymn: 'While humble shepherds watched their flocks'
(R.C.H. 42)

Sermon

Hymn: 'O little town of Bethlehem' (R.C.H. 48)

(*Lights dim towards end of last verse*)
(*This next section could be arranged between choir and
minister, but would be better done with 'voices' distributed
throughout the congregation.*)

Voice 1: Our world is darkened by war-clouds, and by the
shadow of hunger,
ALL: Come, O Christ, and give us light.

Voice 2: We hurt those who love us and quarrels spoil our homes,
ALL: Come, O Christ, and give us light.

Voice 3: We have lost contact with God and our souls are dying,
ALL: Come, O Christ, and give us light.

Voice 4: We have tried in vain to put things right ourselves,
ALL: Come, O Christ, and give us light.

(As near total darkness as possible by this time. A girl's voice sings a lullaby, one verse only. During the next section either candles are lit, or lights go up slowly.)

Voice 1: To you is born this day a Saviour, who is Christ, the Lord.
Choir: Glory to God in the highest.

Voice 2: Unto us a child is born, unto us a son is given and the government shall be upon his shoulder, and his name shall be called: 'WONDERFUL COUNSELLOR, MIGHTY GOD, EVERLASTING FATHER, PRINCE OF PEACE'.
Choir: Glory to God in the highest.

Voice 3: God so loved the world that he gave his only-begotten Son so that whoever believes on him should not perish but have everlasting life.
Choir: Glory to God in the highest.

Voice 4: God has shined in our hearts to give us the light of knowing the glory of God, in the face of Jesus Christ.
Choir: Glory to God in the highest.

Prayer at the Manger
O Living God, before the mystery of a child, born in a stable we bow in awe.
You've come down to our level,
a man among men, lowest of the low, truly 'one of us'.
We cannot understand it,
> but we are grateful that your incredible Love
> is here expressed in flesh and blood,
> so that we might have new life, new love.

Jesus, from your cradle to your grave
      you took people as you found them,
      and you made new people out of them,
So here we are, we are not what we should be,
      we haven't much to offer,
      we're not sure what we believe and what we don't.

But make yourself at home in our lives, Lord,
      even if our lives are as dirty as that stable,
      come in Lord,
      and make something of us, so that we too may be
      able to work for peace and goodwill among men.
For your own love's sake we ask it.   AMEN

Hymn: 'Still the night, holy the night' (R.C.H. 49)

(If there have been candles, then it is during the last verse
of this hymn that the lights could go on.)

THE HANDSHAKE OF PEACE:
(The minister says a basic minimum of what is needed to explain the actual procedure, and the meaning. The easiest
way is for the minister to shake hands with others near him,
who then disperse to various parts of the church, shaking
hands with those at the end of rows, who are asked to pass
it down the pew. It sounds untidy, but has proved very
moving.)

Hymn: 'Love came down at Christmas' (R.C.H. 52)

(This can be sung while the actual handshake is going round.)

Homegoing Prayer
Now, Lord, as we go home,
may your love be shining in our hearts,
so that we may bring happiness to anybody we meet.

May your love in us
make us easier to live with at home,
and better to work with at our work.

May your love in us
enable us to help those who are in need,
and to understand those who are difficult.

May your love in us reach out now
to bless all those in particular need tonight . . .
(*here take in any in special need, local or world-wide*)

Father, into your hands we commit our own lives,
and the lives of our loved ones on earth and in heaven.
Grant us peaceful sleep and joy when we awake,
and now, as one family together we pray:
OUR FATHER . . . . . .

Hymn: 'O Come, all ye faithful' (R.C.H. 55)

Blessing:
Go in peace:
The Wisdom of the Wonderful Counsellor guide you,
The Strength of the Mighty God uphold you,
The Love of the Everlasting Father enfold you,
The Peace of the Prince of Peace be upon you.

And the Blessing of God,
Father, Son and Holy Spirit,
be upon you all this night and for evermore.

Notes:
If a crib or tableau can be arranged, a spot-light could
be focussed on it at midnight, as the lullaby is sung.
If there is a good choir the hymn 'O Come, O Come Immanuel'
(R.C.H. 149) could be sung instead of 'O little town of
Bethlehem" singing as many verses as are needed to bring it
up to midnight.
'Glory to God in the highest' can be borrowed from 'Messiah',
or else the 'Gloria in excelsis deo' from the carol 'Ding Dong
merrily on high' can be used. Organists might make their own
version. A trumpet or two might come in handy here. But, from
experience, it needs careful rehearsal . . . delays and hesita-
tions can spoil the effect. Each member of the choir needs
to have a copy of all the words.
The lullaby at midnight is best done by an unseen singer,
with perhaps one candle to let her see words or music if
necessary. The Gaelic 'Christ-child lullaby', in *Songs
of the Hebrides* by Marjory Kennedy Fraser is ideal here.

4

A CHRISTMAS EVE SERVICE

11 p.m. Community Carol Singing
(*Very relaxed party atmosphere essential. The congregation
is gathering as carol singing proceeds. During the singing
of the final carol candles are lit and all electric lighting
is put out. Hand torches are used by the congregation to read
the hymns. The mood changes sharply as the service begins*)
11.30 p.m. Hymn
Prayer and the Lord's Prayer
Lord, help us to pray.
Many of us don't find it easy;
some of us no longer try
none of us can do it as we ought without your help.
Yet on this night of all nights we want to pray;
to know that you're there,
to know that you hear,
to know that you care.
Help us to realise your presence now not as some shadowy
thing but as the ultimate intimate reality in whom we live
and move and exist, the source of all light and life and
power,
glorious beyond our imagining, yet humble and gentle as a new
born baby in the stable straw.
Help us to talk to you now simply and honestly as children
to their father without constraint or pretence or embarrassment, knowing that if we ask amiss you will give not what we
in our foolishness ask for, but what you in your love and
wisdom know to be best.
Help us to listen to you now, to hear what you are saying to
us not only, as always, through the reading and preaching of
your Word, but also tonight through the darkness and the
silence and, at midnight, through the clamour of voices and
of bells. Hear us and help us through Jesus Christ our Lord.
AMEN

Dear God, you know that part of what we're doing now, even as we try to worship you is only a pretence. Forgive us the pretence that is mere deceit and hypocrisy. But strengthen us in the pretence that is an aspiration to a new and better life. As little children in their games pretend to an adult life they do not understand but long to share, so may we in our worship pretend to that new and better life that you have offered us through Christ. Help us, then, to worship you without hypocrisy and without embarrassment that we may be able to share in the mystery and marvel of the birth of the Holy Child and by his spirit born anew in us may learn to live as we pray. Hear us and help us through Jesus Christ our Lord.   AMEN

OUR FATHER . . . . . .

LESSON

HYMN

SERMON   (7-8 minutes approximately)

HYMN

11.55 p.m. PRAYERS

(*N.B. the length of this prayer must be adjusted to ensure that the singing of the last chord of the carol which follows it coincides precisely with midnight*)

O God, we thank you for the message of *love* that Christmas brings to a world grown hard with hate. Give us in the affairs of men and nations the love that is patient and kind and envies no one; the love that is never boastful nor conceited nor rude; not selfish nor quick to take offence; that in all things we may put love first and so acknowledge the divine right and rule of him who was born at Bethlehem, for love of man made man, Jesus Christ our Lord.

AMEN

O God, we thank you for the message of *joy* that Christmas brings to a world calloused by suffering. We remember in your presence the hungry and destitute millions, your children, our brothers in Christ, who clamour for bread

149

and hope; we remember also those for whom this season is clouded by sickness or anxiety, by over-work or unemployment, by loneliness or bereavement. Keep them from bitterness and despair as they remember the birth of him who bore our griefs and carried our sorrows, yet who was born at Bethlehem that men might have life in all its fullness, Jesus Christ our Lord.   AMEN

O God, we thank you for the message of *peace* that Christmas brings to our distracted world. Give peace among the nations; peace in our land; peace in our homes and peace in our hearts as we remember the birth at Bethlehem of the Prince of Peace, Jesus Christ our Lord.   AMEN

O God, we thank you for the message of *kindness* that Christmas brings to a world grown selfish and cynical through greed. Hear us as we pray for our families and friends that the gifts we receive and give at this time may be true love tokens, symbols of our self-giving in the service of others. So may we all find true joy and fulfilment in giving, as we remember together the birth at Bethlehem of him who came to give himself for us, Jesus Christ our Lord.   AMEN

O God, we thank you for the message of *goodness* that Christmas brings to a world grown sick of sin. Root out from the hearts of all men those things that love darkness rather than light; pride and prejudice, hatred and violence, lust and greed. Strengthen and guide all who strive to build a better world and all who by your grace seek to live a better life that good may prevail over evil, and light over darkness; for the sake of him who was born into the darkness of this world at Bethlehem to be the world's true light; Jesus Christ our Lord.   AMEN

> Come Lord Jesus
>> Where there is hatred, give love,
>> Where there is sadness, give joy,
>> Where there is war, give peace,
>> Where there is greed, give kindness
>> Where there is evil, give goodness

Come Lord Jesus,
> Give light to our darkness, for the hour of your
> birth is near when the bell will ring in the
> silence and the light will shine in the dark.

Come Lord Jesus,
> be born in our hearts through faith,
> that the midnight bell may strike for us the hour
> of grace and your light be our life.

Come Lord Jesus and hear the secret prayer of every
heart
> as we wait for the coming of the morning.

*11.59 p.m. (Part of a hymn or carol may be sung very quietly
by choir or solo voice while the congregation continues in
silent prayer. Alternatively a complete silence may be
observed.)*

Midnight BELL

PRAYER
We bless and adore you, O Christ, Son of God, yet born of
Mary; Son of God, yet our brother; Eternal Word, yet a child
without speech; clothed in glory, yet wrapped in swaddling
bands; Lord of Heaven and earth, yet laid in a manger; strong
in your weakness, glorious in your humility, mighty to save.

Glory be to the Father, and to the Son, and to the Holy
Spirit, as it was in the beginning, is now, and ever shall be,
world without end.

Sung AMEN

*(As the Amen is sung all lights are simultaneously
switched on)*

The minister says:
A Happy Christmas to you all! And now while the choir sings
again to welcome Christmas Morning please greet your neighbours.

*(The 'party' atmosphere of the community singing should
immediately be re-established. The congregation should be encouraged to shake hands or embrace as they would do in their*

own home. The noise and movement will be considerable and the
minister himself should join in. Meantime the bell can be
heard in competition with the choir singing 'Ding dong merrily
on high'.)

As the carol ends the minister says:
As always our first act on Christmas Morning is to remember
the needs of others. Your offering is in aid of . . . . . .

(While the offering is being received very gay music should
be sung or played. A carol sung by the choir with a chorus for
the congregation may be used here.)

Offering Prayer
O God, you have taught us through your Son that when we give
to those in need we give to you also, accept our offering and
use it for your purposes of love, through Jesus Christ our
Lord.

Hymn: 'O come all ye faithful' (R.C.H. 55)
or
'Hark the Herald Angels sing' (R.C.H. 46)

Benediction

Closing Voluntary (Very gay music till all have left the
church.)

5

CHRISTMAS FAMILY SERVICE
(With Communion)

Call to Worship
Behold I bring you good tidings of great joy, which shall
be to all people. For unto you is born . . . in the city of
David a Saviour, who is Christ the Lord . . . Let us now go

to Bethlehem and see this thing which has happened . . . Glory
to God in the highest and on earth his peace for men on whom
his favour rests.

Praise

Prayers (Invocation, Confession, Absolution, Supplication)
O God, in all the gladness we enjoy at the birthday of
your Son, Jesus Christ, we ask you to fill our hearts
with thankfulness and our mouths with songs. In return for
your most wonderful gift we want to offer you the gift of ourselves, to love you and serve you gladly as long as we live.

> O Holy Child of Bethlehem,
>   descend to us, we pray;
> cast out our sin and enter in,
>   be born in us today.
> We hear the Christmas angels
>   the great, glad tidings tell;
> O come to us, abide with us,
>   our Lord Immanuel.

Let us confess to God the wrong things we know we have done.

Dear Father in heaven. You proved you loved us by sending
Jesus to be born like us and among us. We know that we have
not loved you nearly so much as we should, and we have often
been anything but kind and helpful to our fathers and mothers,
our brothers and sisters, not to mention other people. And
we know that this is the real reason why we are often unhappy.

> Lord, have mercy upon us.
> *Christ, have mercy upon us.*
> Lord, have mercy upon us.

Father! We beg you to forgive us, for Jesus' sake. Open our
hearts so that he may be born alive in them; and help us, from
now on, to serve him with all our might, as our Lord and King.

May the Lord Jesus Christ, who shines with the brilliance of
everlasting light, take all darkness right out of our hearts,
now and for ever and ever.   AMEN

Praise

First Lesson   Old Testament:
                   Epistle:

Praise

Second Lesson Gospel:

Intimations

Prayers (Intercessions)
O God, our heavenly Father, who gave your Son to be the Light
of all the world, fill the whole earth with his brightness,
and send his joy and gladness to all fathers and mothers and
boys and girls in every land under the sun.
>   Lord, hear our prayer.
>   *And let our cry come unto you*

We pray for your Church which tells the good news of your
love to everybody. Make all your messengers brave and joyful;
and hurry on the time when everyone shall know that the secret
of happiness is to know you as Lord and King.
>   Lord, hear our prayer.
>   *And let our cry come unto you.*

We pray for boys and girls in Europe and Asia, America, Africa
and Australia, who are glad just as we are at Christmas-time.
Help them to share with others the good news and good gifts
that have come to them because Christ came.
>   Lord, hear our prayer.
>   *And let our cry come unto you.*

We pray for the sick, the suffering and the sad, whether they
are at home or in hospital. Bring them good cheer at this
merry time; and bless the doctors and nurses and all others
who care for them.
>   Lord, hear our prayer.
>   *And let our cry come unto you.*

We pray for our homes, and for our friends and neighbours.
Bless all whom we love who are far away from us: give them

the joy and peace that come from knowing that you are with them
> Lord, hear our prayer.
> *And let our cry come unto you.*

We pray that the radiance of Jesus' presence may shine more and more in the lives of all men, filling them with good-will; and so may every nation receive the gift of peace that he was born to bring.
> Lord, hear our prayer.
> *And let our cry come unto you.*

All these things we ask in his name who lives and reigns with you, O Father, and the Holy Ghost, one God, world without end.

AMEN

Praise

Words of Authority or Prayer for Illumination

Sermon

Ascription

The Creed

The Offering

Invitation

Praise

> The Institution (*N.E.B. or another modern version*)

The Great Prayer:
> The Lord be with you!
> *And also with you!*
> Lift up your hearts!
> *We lift them up unto the Lord.*
> Let us give thanks unto the Lord God!
> *It is meet and right so to do.*

It is right, proper and healthy that we should thank you, God everywhere and always.
For the birth of Jesus your Son, our Saviour, cradled in the manger at Bethlehem:
> *We thank you, heavenly Father.*

For the love and gentle care of Mary, his mother, most blessed of all women:
> *We thank you, heavenly Father.*

For shepherds keeping watch over their flocks by night, who came with haste to worship Christ, the new-born King:
> *We thank you, heavenly Father.*

For wise men from the East, who followed the star and presented him with their gifts of gold and frankinscense and myrrh:
> *We thank you, heavenly Father.*

For the light and love of this Christmas season, in our hearts and in our homes, bringing joy and gladness to us all:
> *We thank you, heavenly Father.*

And in all our joyful gratitude we join our voices with the angels who are always singing to you:
> *Holy, Holy, Holy, Lord God of hosts.*
> *Heaven and earth are full of your glory.*

(Sung)   *Glory be to you, O Lord most high.*
> *Blessed is he that comes in the name of the Lord!*
> *Hosanna in the highest.*

And now, O Lord, we ask you to bless and sanctify these your own gifts of bread and wine that we set before you that they may be to us as the body and blood of Jesus Christ our Lord, so that, eating and drinking them, we may be made one with him and he with us.

And here, in fellowship with your whole Church in heaven and on earth, we offer ourselves to you — all that we have and all that we are; and beg your help so that, being fed at your table, we may surely from now on be better and braver soldiers and servants of our Master, Jesus Christ, in whose words we are bold to pray together, saying:
OUR FATHER . . . . . .

Action

Distribution

Prayers (Thanksgiving, Petition, Commemoration)
Glory to you, O God, in the highest!

Glory to you, Father Almighty, who commanded the light to
shine in the darkness.
Glory to you, O Holy Spirit, always making it possible for us
to live in fellowship with Jesus.
All glory and thanksgiving and power be unto you, O blessed
Trinity, one God for ever and ever.
Blessed Lord Jesus, give us your spirit, we pray. Make us
pure in heart; make our lives all new again, so that we may
bring them to you without having to be too ashamed of them.
Help us to follow the example of your courage and humility
and to serve you by always doing our very best for other
people.
We remember all good, dead people, especially those with whom
we once shared all the joys of Christmas. Keep our love for
them true and steadfast until by your mercy we, along with
them, receive your gift of everlasting life in heaven. And
unto you, O Lord Jesus Christ, with the Father and the Holy
Spirit, be honour and glory for ever and ever.   AMEN

Praise

Benediction

6

THE LAST SUNDAY OF THE YEAR

Lord God, through many days of happy brightness and
through many shadows you have brought us to this hour: often
in the gladsome days we did not thank you for joy, often in
the shadows we blamed you for darkness — we were never alone,
for you were there though we did not recognise you.

Lord, we surrender this year of 19 . . . and give it back to you.
Today we give you our failures, our regrets and our disappoint-
ments, for we have no more use for them: make us now a new
people, eager for the way ahead.
Today we give you all our joys, trusting you to keep them
intact —
most of all we would give you our loyalty, you the God who
challenges men to believe on your Son Jesus, our Master.

Father, we ask no gifts for the year ahead, save only this,
the gift of faith. For the whole world as it now exists,
waiting for the centuries to move ahead and the years to be
counted, our prayer is this: peace between nation and nation,
peace between man and man, peace between me and my heart.

O Lord of all peace, arm us now with courage and resolve,
give us impossible dreams to cherish, and grant us the vision
to see where lies our chiefest joy, through Jesus Christ
our Lord,   AMEN

7

THE FIRST SUNDAY OF THE YEAR

O God, we thank you for bringing us to this new year.

Through you, Father, are all things made new. At this time
especially, we ask that you will forgive our faults in the
past and so cleanse our hearts that we may start again, re-
freshed and renewed to know your will and to do your work
through Christ Jesus, our Lord.

As we stand on the threshold of another year,
encourage us O Father by our few successes of the past;

challenge us, O Christ, to face with fortitude what this year
may bring;
guide us, O Heavenly Spirit, by your eternal presence,
and give us strength to keep our resolutions for the days
to come.

We resolve, O God,
To be true and faithful to those whom we love and who love
us;
To be loyal to our friends, so that they may never feel distressed or let down by our actions;
To work with earnest endeavour, using to the full the talents
which you have given to us;
To be reliable in all our undertakings so that men may take
our word as our bond;
To be temperate in word and action, and to resist temptation
so that we may give strength to others who may be tempted;
To live in full obedience to your will so that in the doing
of it we may find your peace;
To live that our lives may be worthy of Christ, your Son, to
whom with you and the Holy Spirit be all honour, glory and
praise now and for ever.

8

THE PASSION OF OUR LORD

*The readings are from the New English Bible. The
hymns will be sung standing except where marked (tunes in
brackets)*

Hymn (Tallis, R.C.H. 353)
Fair as a beauteous tender flow'r
Amidst the desert grows,

So, slighted by a rebel race,
The heav'nly Saviour rose.

Rejected and despis'd of men,
Behold a man of woe!
Grief was his close companion still
Through all his life below.

Yet all the griefs he felt were ours,
Ours were the woes he bore:
Pangs, not his own, his spotless soul
With bitter anguish tore.

(Paraphrase 25:3-5)

PRAYER

1. Mark 14:12-21: *The Preparation*

Hymn (Tallis) Seated
Thy foes might hate, despise, revile,
Thy friends unfaithful prove:
Unwearied in forgiveness still,
Thy heart could only love. (R.C.H. 87, v. 3)

2. Mark 14:22-26: *The Last Supper*

Hymn (Schmucke dich R.C.H. 324) Seated
Jesus, Bread of Life, I pray thee
Let me gladly here obey thee:
Never to my hurt invited,
Be thy love with love requited:
From this banquet let me measure
Lord, how vast and deep its treasure:
Through the gifts thou here dost give me
As thy guest in heaven receive me.

(R.C.H. 324, v. 4)

3. Mark 14:27-31: *The Mount of Olives*

Hymn (Passion chorale R.C.H. 107)
Protect me, O my Saviour
And keep me close to thee:
Thy power and loving kindness
My strength and stay must be:

O Shepherd, though I follow
Too weak is human will —
But if thou walk beside me
I'll climb the steepest hill.

4. Mark 14:32-42: *The Agony of Jesus*

Hymn (Southwell R.C.H. 102) Seated
Lord Jesus, think on me,
Nor let me go astray
Through darkness and perplexity
Point thou the heavenly way.

(R.C.H. 403, v. 4)

5. Mark 14:43-50: *The Arrest*

Hymn (Southwell) Seated
Lord Jesus, think on me
When flows the tempest high:
When on doth rush the enemy
O Saviour, be thou nigh.

(R.C.H. 403, v. 5)

6. Mark 14:53-65: *The Jewish Trial*

Hymn (Herzliebster Jesu R.C.H. 216) Seated
O Patient Lord,
    when wretched men defy thee,
Reject thy grace,
    thy holy name deny thee:
In willing bonds
    thy perfect love doth tie thee —
For thou wouldst save them!

7. Mark 14:66-72: *Peter's Denial*

Hymn (Southwell SM) Seated
Lord Jesus, think on me
And cleanse me from my sin:
From fear and passion set me free
And make me pure within.

(R.C.H. 403, v. 1 adapted)

8. Mark 15:1-5: *The Roman Trial*

161

Hymn (Passion chorale)
Commit your ways to Jesus
Your fears and anxious care:
The mighty king of heaven
Will every danger share:
The clouds and winds and oceans
All at his bidding flow
His power will make a pathway
Whereon your feet may go.

9. Mark 15:6-14: *The Scourging*

Hymn (Herzliebster Jesu) Seated
O wondrous love,
    that here all shame despising,
Now in our stead
    receives the sharp chastising:
The Master pays
    the debt his servants owe him —
For them is dying!

10. Mark 15:15-21: *The Crown of Thorn*

Hymn (Passion chorale) Seated
O head, so bruised and wounded
Despised, and put to scorn —
O head, by man surrounded
By mocking crown of thorn —
High heaven's host acclaims thee
The Lord all lords above —
O Christ, when mankind shames thee,
I bless thy patient love!

11. Mark 15:22-28: *The Cross*

Hymn (Rockingham, with descant R.C.H. 106) *Seated*
See! from his head, his hands, his feet,
Sorrow and love flow mingled down:
Did e'er such love and sorrow meet,
Or thorns compose so rich a crown?

(R.C.H. 106, v. 3

12. Mark 15:29-32: *Christ Taunted*

Hymn (Passion chorale)
Though men, thy power denying,
So mocked and taunted thee,
It was thy love undying
That nailed thee to the tree:
Thy grief and bitter passion
Were all for sinners' gain:
Mine, mine was the transgression,
But thine the deadly pain.

13. Mark:33-39: *Christ Dies*

Hymn (Rockingham, descant v. 2) Seated
When I survey the wondrous cross
On which the Prince of glory died,
My richest gain I count but loss
And pour contempt on all my pride.

Were the whole realm of Nature mine
That were an offering far too small:
Love so amazing, so divine,
Demands my soul, my life, my all.

(R.C.H. 106, vv. 1, 4)

14. Mark 15:42-47: *The Tomb in the Rock*

Hymn (Misericordia R.C.H. 411)
Just as I am, without one plea
But that thy blood was shed for me
And that thou bid'st me come to thee,
O Lamb of God, I come.

Just as I am, though tossed about
With many a conflict, many a doubt,
Fighting and fears within, without,
O Lamb of God, I come.

Just as I am — thy love unknown
Has broken every barrier down:
Now to be thine, yea thine alone,
O Lamb of God, I come!

AMEN
(R.C.H. 411, vv. 1, 3, 6.)

The Blessing

163

9

THREE HOUR SERVICE, GOOD FRIDAY

(This service is designed in quarter-hour sections.
Each section may be led by a different minister. Only the
order of readings and hymns is suggested, as the ministers
concerned will wish to follow their own procedures within
each section. It is understood that people may come in and
go out as they wish. Plenty of time should be left for
quietness and meditation.)

12.00 noon
Hymn: 'O Come and mourn with me a while'
                    (R.C.H. 96. Tune 'Crosselius', R.C.H. 92)

Is it nothing to you, all you who pass by?
Behold and see if there is any sorrow like my sorrow!
Behold the Lamb of God who takes away the sin of the world

Let us pray
Lord God, as we draw near, under the shadow of the cross,
        grant us insight to understand your sorrow over us,
        grant us insight to see ourselves as you saw us from
            the cross,
        grant us insight to see that a new relationship is
            possible for us in the light of your agony.

Help us to understand why you found us worth agonising.
Help us to see where we cause you agony.
Help us to see our neighbours, and all men as the beloved
    children for whom you died.
May we not go from here without a deeper love in our hearts,
        a deeper love for you,
        a deeper love for all men.

This we ask because of what we see of Jesus on the Cross.
                                                    AMEN

Introductory comment, perhaps reading Isaiah 53.

12.15
Hymn: 'Beneath the Cross of Jesus'((R.C.H. 691)
Luke 23:26-28. 'Weep not for me . . .'

12.30
Hymn: 'Weep not for Him who onward bears' (R.C.H. 94,
Tune 'French', R.C.H. 227)
Luke 23:32-34. 'Father forgive . . .'

12.45
Hymn: 'One who is all unfit to count' (R.C.H. 406)
Mark 15: 22-32. Refusing drugged wine, the mockery.

1.00
Hymn: 'O Sacred Head, sore wounded' (R.C.H. 107)
Luke 23:39-43. 'This day, thou shalt be with me . . .'

1.15
Hymn: 'Lord, when Thy Kingdom comes, remember me'
(R.C.H. 98. Tune 'Ellers', R.C.H. 301)
John 19:25-27. 'Woman, behold your son . . .'

1.30
Hymn: 'What grace, O Lord, and beauty shone' (R.C.H. 87)
Mark 15:33-34. 'Eloi . . .'

1.45
Hymn: 'Throned upon the awful Tree' (R.C.H. 100. Tune
'Petra', R.C.H. 413)
John 19:28-29. 'I thirst'

2.00
Hymn: 'His are the thousand sparkling rills' (R.C.H. 101.
Tune 'Saffron Walden', R.C.H. 497)
John 19:30a. 'It is finished'

2.15
Hymn: 'O perfect life of love!' (R.C.H. 102. Tune
'Selma', R.C.H. 249)
Luke 23:46. 'Father, into thy hands . . .'

2.30
Hymn: 'When I survey the wondrous Cross' (R.C.H. 106)
Mark 15:37-39.

2.45
Hymn: 'My faith looks up to Thee' (R.C.H. 415)
Mark 15:42-47. The burial.

3.00
Hymn: 'Dark the day on Calvary's Cross' (R.C.H. 112.
Tune 'Pascal', R.C.H. 413)

Note on hymns:
Most hymn-books have excellent hymns which are seldom, if ev
used because their tunes are unknown. Very often the words ar
more appropriate than the usual hymns and the people appreci
them more when they are sung to well-known tunes.

10

AN EASTER EUCHARIST

Introit: This joyful Eastertide (Kingsway Carol
Book, No. 4)

The Lord is risen.
The Lord is risen indeed. Alleluia!

Hymn: Alleluia! Alleluia! Alleluia!
    The strife is o'er, the battle done: (R.C.H. 122)

Christ our paschal lamb has been sacrificed for us; so let
us keep festival.
Christ being raised from the dead will never die again;
death no longer has dominion over him.
Thanks be to God who gives us the victory through our Lord
Jesus Christ.

166

Let us pray
You, Lord the Father, we praise. You raised our Lord Jesus
from the dead. We wonder at your power.
You, Lord the Son, we praise. You are alive always, and are
among us now. We exult in your victory.
You, Lord the Spirit, we praise. You give us the gladness and
assurance of faith. We delight in your bounty.
You, Lord the Trinity, we praise. Glory and thanksgiving be
yours, never ending.

Lord Jesus, in your risen splendour, we adore you.
You have broken the power of sin. You have burst the bonds
of death.
Let joy abound in us; let joy abound in all the Church.
Let joy assail the darkness of the world; let joy irradiate
creation.
Let the saints in heaven rejoice; let the angelic choirs
rejoice; let joy ascend about the throne of God.

Holy God, our joy is shadowed by our sin.
We have not truly absorbed the message of Christ's victory.
> We tremble at life.
> We shudder at death.
> We succumb to gloom and despair.
> We slump into grief and remorse.
> We have been apathetic and lethargic.
> We have lacked spiritual zest and moral passion.
>> Lord, have mercy.
>> *Christ, have mercy.*
>> Lord, have mercy.

Accept, dear people, assurance of forgiveness.
Listen to the Word of God:
Here are words you may trust, words that merit full acceptance
'Christ Jesus came into the world to save sinners.'

As a minister of Christ, I address to you who are truly
penitent the Lord's absolution: Your sins are forgiven; go
in peace.
> Lord, will you not give us new life;
> *That your people may rejoice in you?*

Lord, show us your true love;
And grant us your deliverance.
Lord, hear our prayer;
And let our cry for help reach you.

Lord, give us the power of new life.
Give us faith, faith to secure us victory over doubt
and adversity.
Give us love, love to bind us to you and to one
another.
Give us hope, hope to help us look beyond the
tumults of this world to the peace and tranquillity
of the world to come.
All this we ask in Jesus' name, who lives and reigns with you,
Father, in the unity of the Spirit, one God, always.

AMEN

Hymn: 'Jesus Christ is risen today,

Hallelujah!' (R.C.H. 119)

Let us pray
God our Father, grant that as we joyfully celebrate the
mysteries of the resurrection of our Lord Jesus Christ, so,
in the world to come, we may, with all your saints, rejoice
in the revelation of your glory; through him who loved us
and washed us from our sins in his own blood, and who now
lives and reigns with you and the holy Spirit, one God,
always.
Let your Word, Lord, bring us light and joy in the gospel;
through Christ our Saviour.

AMEN

Lections: Isaiah 12:1-6;
Revelation 1:12-18.

Metrical Psalm: 'O sing a new song to the Lord'
(No. 98:1-6)

Lection: St Mark 16:1-8.

Hymn: 'Hallelujah! Hallelujah!
Hearts to heaven and voices raise' (R.C.H. 126)

Intimations

Sermon

Ascription of Glory

Te Deum (to a modern setting)

Let us pray
Almighty Father, hear our prayers for the Church and the
world which we offer in the name of him who lives and intercedes for us, our Saviour Jesus Christ.

Let us pray for the Church:
Lord, whose rule alone can bring joy to the world: fill your
Church with the power of the risen Christ, that it may live
in steadfast obedience to your will. Deepen its faith;
enliven its witness; and impel it to reach out and gather
mankind into your kingdom; through him who died and was raised
for us all, our Saviour Jesus Christ.
> Lord, hear our prayer;
> *And let our cry for help reach you.*

Let us pray for the Church of Scotland:
Lord, by whose providence the Church has been planted in our
land: we pray for the parishes of Scotland, that love and
zeal for the Lord Jesus may grow among our people; and for
our ministers, that they may preach the word and celebrate
the sacraments with learning, ardour, and skill; through him
who is the Head Shepherd of our souls, our Saviour Jesus
Christ.
> Lord, hear our prayer;
> *And let our cry for help reach you.*

Let us pray for the unity of the Church:
Grant, Almighty God, that all who love the Lord Jesus may
be so drawn to one another in unity of mind and heart that
they may manifest to the world a unity in faith and life: to
the joy of the same Lord Jesus who prayed that all his followers
might be one, that the world might believe.
> Lord, hear our prayer;
> *And let our cry for help reach you.*

Let us pray for those Christians who suffer persecution:
Lord God, who are always the strength and refuge of your
people: uphold all who suffer for their allegiance to Christ.
Give them faith and courage to endure; and may they by their
witness and example win others for the service of him who
suffered for all mankind, our Saviour Jesus Christ.

   Lord, hear our prayer;
   And let our cry for help reach you.

Let us pray for the world's rulers:
Lord, in whose hand are the destinies of the nations: we
pray for all who exercise the power of government over the
peoples. Make them defenders of liberty and champions of
justice; and so rule in their hearts that they may also be
lovers and makers of peace; through him who is the Prince of
Peace, our Saviour Jesus Christ.

   Lord, hear our prayer;
   And let our cry for help reach you.

Let us pray for our country:
Lord, who alone are truly sovereign over this people: make
the life of this nation subject to your will in Christ, that
unity and harmony, compassion and brotherhood may grow and
flourish, and that the Jerusalem of dreams may be built among
us; through him who is the sure foundation, our Saviour Jesus
Christ.

   Lord, hear our prayer;
   And let our cry for help reach you.

Let us pray for the royal family:
Lord, from whom all dignities come: we pray for Elizabeth
our Queen, Philip Duke of Edinburgh, Charles Prince of Wales
and Duke of Rothesay, and all the members of the royal house.
Uphold them amid the onerous round of public duty; make them
equal to every claim that is made upon them; and establish
their lives in him who can be the strength of our life, our
Saviour Jesus Christ.

   Lord, hear our prayer;
   And let our cry for help reach you.

Let us pray for the Queen's ministers and all who share in
government:
Lord, to whom all who weild power are accountable: we pray
for the Prime Minister, the members of the Cabinet, and all
in Parliament. Guide their understanding and prompt their
judgement, that they may order our affairs with wisdom and
resourcefulness. Foster in them a loyalty to your law, which
is embodied in our Saviour Jesus Christ.
> Lord, hear our prayer;
> *And let our cry for help reach you.*

Let us pray for all in trouble:
Lord, from whom come life and joy: we commend to your healing
and comfort all who are in sickness or sorrow of any kind.
We remember especially those known to us . . . . . . We name them
now in our hearts before you . . . . . . Undergird them with your
presence; give them patience and fortitude; and let your power
to restore and renew be strong within them; through him who
is the Great Physician, our Saviour Jesus Christ.
> Lord, hear our prayer;
> *And let our cry for help reach you.*

Let us remember with thanksgiving the faithful departed:
Lord our God, whose wonderful grace the Church triumphant is
always extolling: we thank you for the splendid company of
apostles, saints, and martyrs who have served you faithfully
here, and who now rejoice in the glory of heaven.
Grant that with them we may share in the victory of Christ,
and with them, at the last, perfectly praise and adore you.
All this we ask, Lord, in the name of Christ, who lives and
reigns with you and the holy Spirit, one God, always.

AMEN

Creed

Offering

*(The celebrant receives the offering at the holy table.
The liturgy of the word being ended, the liturgy of the
faithful now begins.)*

Dear people, hear St Paul's account of the institution of
the Lord's Supper:
For the tradition which I handed on to you came to me from
the Lord himself: that the Lord Jesus, on the night of his
arrest, took bread and, after giving thanks to God, broke it
and said: 'This is my body, which is for you; do this as a
memorial of me.' In the same way, he took the cup after
supper, and said: 'This cup is the new covenant sealed by
my blood. Whenever you drink it, do this as a memorial of
me.' For every time you eat this bread and drink the cup,
you proclaim the death of the Lord, until he comes.

Dear people, it is good that we should remember that this
sacrament is a memorial of the sacrifice of Christ for the
sins of men, a means of grace to those who believe in him,
and a bond and pledge of their union with him, and with each
other as members of his mystical body.
Therefore it is necessary that we come with knowledge, faith,
repentance, and love; not holding fellowship with evil, or
cherishing pride or self-righteousness, but, conscious of our
weakness and in sorrow for our sins, humbly putting our
trust in Christ, and seeking his grace.

Draw near to the holy table, and hear the gracious words of
the Lord Jesus:

I am the bread of life. Whoever comes to me shall never be
hungry, and whoever believes in me shall never be thirsty.
The man who comes to me I will never turn away.

> The peace of the Lord be with you.
> *And also with you.*

Hymn: 'And now, O Father, mindful of the love' (R.C.H. 320)

*(During the hymn, the offering is removed, and the elements
of bread and wine are brought to the holy table.)*

Let us pray.
Holy Father, by the blood of your dear Son you have opened
up a new and living way into your presence: we come to you,
unworthy as we are, praying that you will accept us, and
these your gifts, for your glory. All that is in heaven and

on earth belongs to you, Lord, and of your own we give you;
through Christ your Son.

AMEN

As the Lord Jesus, the night he was arrested, took bread, I
take these elements of bread and wine to be set apart from
all common uses to this holy use and mystery; and as he gave
thanks, let us draw near to God, and present to him our
prayers and thanksgivings.

> The Lord be with you.
> *And also with you.*
> Lift up your hearts.
> *We lift them up to the Lord.*
> Let us give thanks to our Lord God.
> *It is right and good that we should.*

It is truly right and good that we should at all times and
in all places give thanks to you, Lord, Holy Father, Almighty,
Everlasting God, who made the world and man, and whose love
and goodness enfold creation.
Especially this day we praise you for Jesus Christ, the true
paschal Lamb, who has taken away the sin of the world, and
opened the gate of heaven to all who believe.
With angels and archangels and all the company of heaven, we
acclaim you, with exultant voice, praising you and saying:

> *Holy, holy, holy, Lord God of hosts,*
> *Heaven and earth are full of your glory:*
> *Glory belongs to you, Lord most high.*

Holy you are, Lord, holy and bountiful: you loved the world
so much that you gave your only Son, that everyone who has
faith in him may not die, but have eternal life.
Not as we should, but as we can, we thank you for his wonderful birth, his pure and compassionate life, his atoning death,
his triumphant resurrection, his promised coming again, and
his gift of the holy Spirit.
Remembering what he was and what he did, we offer
you this memorial of him. Through the holy Spirit hallow both
us and these gifts of your creation, that the bread which

we break may be the communion of the body of Christ and the
cup which we bless the communion of the blood of Christ, that
we, receiving them, may by faith share in his body and blood,
with all his blessings, to our spiritual nourishment and
growth in grace.
And here we give you ourselves, all that we are, to be a
living sacrifice. We ask you to accept this sacrifice of
thanksgiving, and we pray that all the faithful may be filled
with your presence and power; through Jesus Christ our Lord,
by whom and with whom, in the unity of the Spirit, all
praise and glory be yours, Lord God, heavenly Father, now and
always.
As our Saviour taught us, we are bold to pray, saying:
OUR FATHER . . . . . .

According to the holy institution, example, and command of
our Lord Jesus Christ, and for a memorial of him, we do
this: who, on the night of his arrest, took bread
    (Here the celebrant takes bread into his hands)
and, after giving thanks to God, broke it,
    (here he breaks the bread)
and said: 'This is my body, which is for you; do this as a
memorial of me.'
In the same way, he took the cup after supper,
    (here he raises the cup)
and said: 'This cup is the new covenant sealed by my blood.
Whenever you drink it, do this as a memorial of me.'

    Lamb of God, you take away the sin of the world:
    have mercy on us.
    Lamb of God, you take away the sin of the world:
    give us your peace.

*(After the celebrant has communicated, he delivers the bread
and wine to the people.)*
    In giving the bread, he says:
This is the body of Christ, which is for you; do this as a
memorial of him.

    In giving the wine, he says:

174

This cup is the new covenant sealed by the blood of Christ.
Whenever you drink it, do this as a memorial of him.

When all have communicated, the celebrant says:

Let us pray
Heavenly Father, we thank you for bringing us into communion
with our risen Saviour, and with all who love him in heaven
and on earth; and we pray that, mindful of his love and
strengthened by his grace, we may serve you faithfully all
our days; through Jesus Christ our Lord.
Lord Christ, send us out to make known your Gospel and to
build up your Kingdom: you who live and reign with the
Father and the holy Spirit, one God, always.

AMEN

Hymn: 'Now may He who from the dead' (R.C.H. 300)

Go in the peace of Christ to serve him in the world. The
grace of the Lord Jesus Christ, and the love of God, and the
fellowship of the holy Spirit be with you, always.

AMEN

*While the bread and wine are removed from the church, the
people may sing,*
Paraphrase: 'The Saviour dy'd, but rose again' (No. 48:5-9)

11

A GENERAL INTERCESSION FOR THE DAY OF PENTECOST

Holy and Almighty God,
your Holy Spirit is at work in the Church
    to enlighten,
    to comfort,
    and to guide:

175

Send your life-giving Spirit into the Church in Scotland, we
pray, so that men may know that you are with your Church.
Help the Church to make public the good news of your love
in every corner of Scotland,
and in every corner of the world,
until all the people hear it in their own language,
     and praise you in their own language,
     and rejoice to know of your love.

God of our Father,
we ask you now to do good to our country;
we see the Holy Spirit at work throughout our history,
     guiding us,
     leading us,
     sometimes rebuking us.
Continue to help us by the Holy Spirit, so that our life
together may be the life your people ought to live.

God of love, and God of peace,
may the power of your Holy Spirit be seen in the world:
may knowledge of your truth overcome the pride, anger and
greed which make men strive against each other;
may knowledge of your truth guide and strengthen those who
represent the people of the world in international discussion,
so that justice, mercy and peace may be victorious.
Lead all the nations in the way of good will and common
service, and bind the whole family of man in one unbroken
brotherhood, in the kingdom of your Son.

Father,
you know the needs of all your children; send the comfort of
the Holy Spirit, we pray, to all in trouble.
Strengthen the weak,
uphold the sick,
refresh the weary,
bring new hope to those who are in despair,
and strong consolation to those who mourn.

Everywhere, and in every way, let your will be done, Father,
through Jesus Christ our Lord.

                                 AMEN

12
AFTER PENTECOST

I.
Jesus said, 'I will not leave you to face life all alone . . .
The Spirit will come . . .'

Lord God, such great news this is!
Truly you are the living God . . .
Truly you are not dead, but risen in power . . .
Truly you have not left us; instead you are accompanying us;
the Spirit has come!

Such great news this is!
This makes all the difference in the world.

Come, Spirit of Jesus, come as you promised;
  to us, gathered together in your name, come Spirit
  of Jesus,
  to those of us who feel happy and at peace with the
  world, come Spirit of Jesus,
  to those of us who feel troubled, full of worries,
  surrounded by problems, come Spirit of Jesus,
  to those of us who feel eager for life and for the
  future, come Spirit of Jesus,
  to those of us who feel tired and done, with only
  memories to keep us going, come Spirit of Jesus,
  to those of us who feel close to you, sure of you,
  come Spirit of Jesus,
  to those of us who feel very unsure, with very
  little faith, come Spirit of Jesus,
  to old and young, to each and all, in this place,
  in this hour, come Spirit of Jesus.
Help us to worship, to sing, pray, think, and give of ourselves.
Because of your promise we ask this.

II.

O God, Father and friend to us, we give thanks!
O Jesus, Saviour and leader to us, we give thanks!
O Holy Spirit, Comforter and life-giver to us, we give thanks!
O God, coming to us in so many forms and ways, yet always
the same, always true, always yourself, we give thanks!

Today, if your word has become clearer to us, got through
to us, we thank you.
If your promise has at last convinced us, and we have begun
to trust you, we thank you.
If your presence has really touched us, and we have felt a
new peace of mind, we thank you.

Realising our privileges, we realise the problems and needs
of others

     how frightening life must be for those who do not
     know you as a God of love;
     how pointless life must be for those who live only
     for money and possessions;
     how desperate life must be for those who have been
     hit by war and by disaster, like the people
     of . . . . . .;
     how lonely life must for people who have to make
     life-or-death decisions, that affect the fate of
     others;
     how difficult life must be for people seriously ill,
     and for their families, for homes where there is
     tension between husband and wife, parents and
     children, for men out of work, for those who are
     trying to face the death of one who means everything
     in the world to them.
In quietness, we think of these people . . . . . .

Use the Church, and use us, to help where we can, and so
continue the service, the prayer, the faithful living of the
men and women of the Spirit of long ago and of our own time
and of our own family circles, giving honour and glory to
you, the one God, Father, Son and Holy Spirit, blessed for
ever.

13

PRAYERS FOR ALL SAINTS

'How blest are those whose hearts are pure;
they shall see God.
How blest are the peacemakers; God shall call them
his sons.
How blest are those who have suffered persecution
for the cause of right; the kingdom of heaven is
theirs.'

(I)
Let us offer to God our prayers of Adoration, Confession and
Supplication.

Let us pray
God, the eternal, the creator, the refuge and strength of your
people in all ages; one generation has praised your works to
another and spoken of your involvement in human history. We
have heard what our fathers have declared and we, their
children, worship you now — a witness to your faithfulness
and in praise of your name.

Lord our God, your compassion does not fail; we acknowledge
that we do not merit our worldly prosperity, nor your mercy,
and we confess our debts to society and to you. We have broken
our vows as Christians and church members. We have not been
faithful to Jesus and those who strove manfully to follow
him; we have forgotten their example; we have been unfaithful
to the trust committed to us.

Forgive us, Father; and make us worthier of the apostles,
their followers — the faithful in every age — and the inheritance we have received from them. Grant that the
good we have seen and felt in them may inspire and guide us.
And with all these witnesses around us like a cloud, let us
throw off every encumbrance, every sin to which we cling,

and run with resolution the race for which we are entered,
our eyes fixed on Jesus, on whom our faith depends from start
to finish that we indeed may be found faithful in this world,
and in the world to come receive the unfading crown of glory.

O God our creator, you have bound us all into one fellowship
in Jesus Christ our Lord; give us grace to follow the faithful
of all ages in a life of virtue and godliness, that we may
come at the last to those unknown joys which you have prepare
for those who love you.

In Christ's name,   AMEN

(II)
Let us offer to God our prayers of intercession and thanksgiving.

Let us pray

God, you have founded a church upon earth and have revealed
your loving and kindness and truth in every age. We ask you
to make your people everywhere rich in grace. Keep them true
to the heritage of faith received from those who have gone
before. Help them to serve you in righteousness and reverence.
Unite them in their discipleship of Jesus. May they experience
the fellowship of the faithful of this and every age.

Bless your church in our native land. Pour out your spirit on
its members to cherish received traditions and to make new
ventures of faith according to your will.

Bless our Queen and her house as she goes in our name to
other countries. As we hear of her journeyings, make us
aware of the poverty of potential greatness of these nations;
make us mindful that they are our brothers in Christ and that
they, too, thave their gift to offer to mankind.

Bless our rulers, the high court of parliament, who govern
in the Queen's name. May they seek to serve the nation and
the wider community of the world, eschewing fame, fortune
and personal power.

Merciful Father, seek the lost sheep and bring them back to
the fold. Look in compassion on the sick, the suffering and
the distressed; so order the world that their needs may be

met and make us mindful of the part we must play in seeing
that your will is done. Hear us, especially for those whom
we now name in the silence of our hearts . . . . . .
Comfort them with your love.

Eternal Father — God not of the dead, but of the living — we
thank and praise you for the faithful of all generations who
served you in godliness and love, and are now with you in
glory.

We thank you for those who have enriched the world with truth
and beauty — for the wise and good of every land and age.
Teach us to follow them as they followed Christ; that at
the last we may receive with them the prize of eternal life.
Through Jesus, the Christ, our Lord.   AMEN

14

SERVICES AND PRAYERS FOR CIVIC OCCASIONS

The Kirkin' of the Council
I.
Unless the Lord builds the house, its builders will have
toiled in vain.
Unless the Lord keeps watch over a city, in vain the watchman
stands on guard.
Our help is in the name of the Lord, maker of heaven and earth.

Praise the Lord, who came mysteriously to create life.
Praise the Lord, who came mercifully to save life.
Praise the Lord, who comes energetically to make life new.
Praise the Lord — Creator, Saviour, Life-giver — for our help
is in him.

Lord God, so wonderfully you have made us, so generously you have blessed us.
Alongside your majesty, we feel small.
Alongside your wisdom, we feel foolish.
Alongside your grace and love, we feel failures.

It is tempting to look away from you and to focus only on ourselves, to persuade ourselves of our power and wisdom, our honesty and good judgement, to believe we can build well enough, keep watch easily, without help.

Show us ourselves, our problems, our powers and our possibilities, in perspective, and at this time of fresh beginnings, help us to put our trust in you, whom we can rely on, and with whom we will be safe, always.

II.
Sing to the Lord, and bless his name.
Declare among the nations, 'The Lord is King'.

Lord God, above the limitations of time and space, yet with us always . . . splendid as the King of kings, yet once a man like us . . . we come with worship and praise. May it be genuine, and fit for a king, and a strength to each one of us in this place.

Gracious Lord, you know us better than we know ourselves: the heights we can rise to and the depths we can sink to, our possibilities and our limitations, our achievements and our downfalls.
We come with embarrassment, and we ask for pardon . . .
We come with anxiety about the future, and we ask for a quiet mind . . .
We come uncertain, and we ask for guidance . . .
We come unsure of ourselves, and we ask for support . . .
We come with a sense of responsibility, and we ask for a blessing . . .

Mighty and wise Lord, you know what is needed, and you can do it, in us and for us. Accept us, with our needs and our prayers. Give us the faith to trust, the impulse to serve, and the courage to go on, now and always.

III.

Lord God, you have given us life, and a share in the uncovering
and extending of its blessings: we praise you for your gifts
and we pray for your help to use them rightly.

We give thanks for the freedom and safety in which we live:
for peaceful homes, justice and order in our society, standards
of truth and honour, and for all our rights and freedoms.

And we pray for those whose work is to maintain and extend
these blessings: all who are given authority and responsibility
among us; for Elizabeth our Queen and the members of the
Royal Family; for the High Court of Parliament and those who
represent us there; for the (Lord) Provost, Magistrates,
Councillors and officials of this city (town); and for all
who with them have the care of this city's life, in administer-
ing the law and keeping the peace, in education and the care
of children, in planning and building, in providing both
for work and leisure. Direct and use their influence, that
we may help build a neighbourhood and a community whose life
does honour to your name.

We give thanks for the blessings of daily work: for the chance
to work and earn our daily bread, and for all we owe to those
whose work brings us what we need, especially those whose
work by land or sea is dangerous or unpleasant.

And we pray for the working life of our world and of our
city (town): for those who direct it and carry it out; those
who strive to maintain good standards of craftmanship; and
those who attempt to lift from it the drabness and insecurity
that deaden man's spirit.

We remember those who are out of work, because of ill-health
or because their skill is not wanted, and we pray for the
building of good relations in industry. Grant us the ability
so to plan that men and women may be able to find in their
work dignity, justice, and a service to others, after the
example of Jesus Christ.

We give thanks for the blessings of family life and of the
care which daily surrounds us: for good health and all the
opportunities and hopes that are open to us.

And we pray for those who give their skill to the health and welfare of the community, those who care for the ill in body or mind, and all who by thoughtfulness and sympathy help to mend broken lives. We remember those who are denied such blessings: the permanently hungry and homeless across the world, those who are oppressed and enslaved, and we pray for justice and generosity in our time for them. And we remember those in our own neighbourhood and friendship who are sufferi who are giving up hope, whose illness human skill cannot cure; and families where death and sorrow has come.

The unsolved problems, the unanswered questions, we bring to you, O God, that through us you may come and heal and bless, in the way of Jesus Christ.

We give thanks above all for the understanding to pray, for a place to pray, for the faith to pray; for the mighty victory of your Son our Saviour Jesus Christ; and for all who in this city and across the world have kept this faith, that we might know it and live by it. We praise you for the servants of God down the ages who have caught the vision of a city of which you are architect and builder, the goal of all human history and hope. We ask a place among the faithful ones, and help to do our part in our day, that the vision may grow clearer, and the day of its dawning draw closer, and your kingdom finally come.
And to you be the glory.

The Opening of the Town Council
Lord God, we believe all power and authority is from you: we praise you for your gifts, and for a way of life that encourages men and women to put their talents at the service of others, and at this time we offer ourselves to serving the good of this city.

Teach us how to use the power that has been lent us; show us how to translate power into service, how to wield authority with humility.

Teach us when to be cautious, and when to be bold; teach us both how to speak and how to listen; teach us how to distingui between what is important and what is not.

O God, empower us for what lies waiting to be done, guide
us in the doing of it, and uphold us until it is completed.
And in it all may there be honour and glory to you, through
Jesus Christ our Lord.

Law and Order
Almighty God, to whom we owe our sense of truth and honour,
our striving after what is just and right, steady us and guide
us in our using of these gifts. Grant that in carrying out
the responsibilities that lie before us, the cause of truth
may be upheld, human weakness corrected and strengthened,
the community safeguarded, and your name honoured; through
Jesus Christ our Lord.

Remembrance Day
I.
Jesus said:

> How blest are those who know their need of God . . .
> How blest are those who show mercy . . .
> How blest are those who long to see the right
> prevail . . .
> How blest are the peacemakers . . .

O God of power, we worship you.
Though life be insecure, though courage fail, though the
future be uncertain, there is no change in you, no wavering
in your purpose.
We know our need of you: give us your blessing.

O God of mercy, we worship you.
So much we promised to do, and it is still not done.
So much that is cruel and wicked still goes unchecked in our
society.
So many in this world are still enslaved and uncared for.
Conscience-stricken and ashamed, we would try to show mercy:
be merciful to us.

O God of hope, we worship you.
The issues before us frighten us, the problems seem so great,
and our resources so small.

185

We would be peacemakers; we long to see the right prevail.
Keep your promises; give us your blessings; help us to see
your will, and lead us out to obey it; through Jesus Christ
our Lord.

II.
Almighty God, we remember with thankfulness this day all
that makes life secure and blessed: the freedom from war and
want that we have; the chance to rebuild and recreate even
after devastation and suffering.

We remember with pride those whose lives have channelled
these gifts of yours into our history: those who have built
and planned with inspiration and vision; those who have
defied the enemies of progress and freedom; those who have
fought and died to keep all this safe for generations to come.

We remember with reverence him who made these things possible
and worth striving for, who gave us hope, both in life and
in death — your Son our Saviour, Jesus Christ.

As we remember what has been done for us, we recognise also
what this world still lacks, still cries for, still must
have if your will is to be done.

We remember peoples still locked in tension and strife, still
divided by bitterness and intolerance,

We remember those who are still oppressed because of their
colour, their race, their beliefs,

We remember those who are denied a full life because of the
wounds they bear on body and mind, and those to whom this
day has brought great sadness and loneliness,
— and we pray for their peace . . .

We remember those who hold themselves ready to keep the
peace of the community and of the nations, and those who
protest and speak out for those who cannot speak for themselves,
— and we pray for their vigilance . . .

We remember those who shape the policies of nations, who can
build or destroy with a word, and those who seek to unite
the imaginations of others in the cause of freedom and truth,

We remember our gracious Queen, the High Court of Parliament, and those who represent us there; the Lord Provost, Magistrates, Councillors and officials of this city (town),

We remember the working life of our land and our community, and those who in (Incorporated Trades), Chamber of Commerce, and Trades Council, seek to plan wisely, to maintain standards, and to share the benefits of life to each and all, — and we pray for their upholding . . .

And we pray for ourselves: that we may not only think noble thoughts and mean well this day.
Take our gifts, our strength, our vision, our hope, and mould them by the power of your Spirit, until we see your purpose, and do your will, and seek your kingdom for this world of your making; by the grace of Jesus Christ, to whom with you, O Father, and the Holy Spirit, be all might, majesty, dominion and power, world without end.

15
THE KIRKING OF THE LORD PROVOST, MAGISTRATES AND COUNCILLORS

Call to prayer
A craftsman is recognised by his skilful hand and a councillor by his words of wisdom. Wise rulers make a city fit to live in. In the Lord's hand is all human success. The origin of pride is to forsake the Lord.

Prayer
O God, in whose presence we find ourselves wherever truth and goodness, love and inspiration are to be found: help us thy servants to call to mind every event in the week that is

past in which we should have discerned thy presence; and in thanksgiving both for the good we have received, and for the evil which has failed to conquer us, may we give unto thee, Lord of all life, worship and adoration; through Jesus Christ our Lord.

O God, who has called us in Jesus Christ to live in this world as citizens of a perfect kingdom that is to come: we confess all that is wrong in our own personal lives, and our failure to create a society in which all men have freedom of opportunity to grow according to thy purpose in knowledge and grace. We confess that we are very ready to lay the blame on other people and to excuse ourselves. Grant us grace, we pray thee, to see ourselves with all our faults; to have an honest desire to amend our ways; and to have unshakeable confidence in thy power to help and save; through Jesus Christ our Lord.

O almighty God, who alone canst order the unruly wills and affections of sinful men: grant unto thy people that they may love the thing which thou commandest, and desire that which thou dost promise; that so, among the sundry and manifold changes of the world, our hearts may surely there be fixed, where true joys are to be found; through Jesus Christ our Lord.

* * *

Intercessions

O thou whose kingdom is without territories yet covers all lands, whose realm is without boundaries yet crosses all frontiers:
Extend thy rule over human hearts and break down all barriers which keep mankind divided.
Grant to the nations of the world the saving knowledge of thy love, so that there may be one kingdom of righteousness and truth in which all peoples may praise thy glorious name.

Almighty God, hear us as we pray to thee for the nation to which we belong. Guide with thy eternal wisdom our Queen and

her counsellors. Protect her especially in her journeys abroad
that she may be a blessing to her peoples.

Almighty God, from whom cometh every good gift; give to the
Lord Provost, the magistrates and councillors of this city,
the spirit of justice and integrity, of wisdom and understanding; that seeking to serve the well-being of those whom they
represent, they may ever advance thy kingdom in this place
and promote the real welfare of thy people.

O God the Creator of all, who hast set in every person the
image of thyself: Have mercy upon all who are unemployed;
and help us so to order our life that every man may find work
and joy in doing it.

Have mercy, we pray, on any who have no homes; or whose houses
are miserable and lacking those necessities which we enjoy in
ours. Bless all who work to help them, and keep our conscience
ever awake until we have found every answer to their problems.

O God, we pray that thou wilt help us to build a city beautiful,
prosperous, and concerned for citizen and stranger, with
nothing that is a barrier to true fellowship, so that more
and more, as we draw nearer to thee our Father, we may become
thy family in this place.

Now unto the Father, the Son, and the Holy Spirit be honour,
glory, and dominion, world without end.

16
A SERVICE FOR YOUTH ORGANISATIONS

Opening Prayers
O God, powerful and wise, just and loving, all that the
best of fathers ought to be, we have come to say in this
service that we are not wise enough or strong enough to live
without thy help.
We do not claim to understand thee or to be able to prove to
other people that thou art here and everywhere. We do not
claim that we have no doubts.
But we believe that Jesus Christ was one to be trusted above
all others. He calls us to love thee and serve thee and to
believe in thy power to help in all our needs.

Forgive us, O God, for all that is wrong or weak or squalid
in the way we think or speak or behave. We who try to follow
Christ are often jealous, resentful, and bitter against
others. We offend and hurt other people, we break our promises
and let thee down.

Help us to see our faults and make amends where we can. Help
us to believe so much in thy love that we shall feel secure
enough to get no pleasure from looking down on others or
hurting them. So may we be at peace with thee, with other
people, and with ourselves; through Jesus Christ our Lord.

*   *   *

Intercessions
We pray, O God, for thy Church in all the world, that it may
show Christ to all men. Where Christians meet let men see
that they are not divided by colour or class or politics;
and, even though they do not believe all the same things or

worship in exactly the same way, may it be seen that their united love for thee is greater than all their differences.

We pray for everyone who is made to suffer imprisonment, loss of work, or lack of friends because he tries to follow Christ and will not go with the crowd. Make such people strong-willed and cheerful that others may be attracted to faith like theirs.

We pray for this country of ours with its great traditions of strength, wisdom, and skill, ever ready to help the weak and the needy. Here may we conquer all who laugh at goodness, who sneer at fair play, who call evil good. Here may we bring to an end the efforts of all who try to live by violence or who try to cheat others by cunning schemes.

May we reward good service, faithful work, and recognise true worth.

Lead every nation to a peaceful and fair settlement of its problems, we pray, and help all men to live as thy family, sharing the world's resources, and bearing each other's burdens.

We pray for the homes in which we and our neighbours live, that in them love like thine may be found, husbands and wives, parents and children with a spirit of understanding, ready to forgive, places filled with joy and peace.

We pray for everyone who is ill. Make them strong and cheerful in spirit, and bring them recovery, if it be possible, through the skill and care of doctors and nurses, and through people like ourselves may thy presence become real to them; through Jesus Christ our Lord.

17

A HARVEST THANKSGIVING SERVICE

Introduction
This service is built up on readings, and depends for its
effect on having two good readers who have been rehearsed
beforehand. Each should have a typed copy of the passages to
be read because the readings will be too long if they are
not condensed. A linking narrative and comment should be given
by the minister.

Hymn: 'Come ye thankful people come' (R.C.H. 619)

> Let the people praise God
> Let all the nations praise Him.
> For the earth has yielded its fruit
> and God, even our God, has blessed us.

Let us pray
O God, Our God,
as thy family we gather before thee at thy table,
as brothers and sisters in Christ we come to rejoice before thee,
as part of the worldwide family we come to sing thy praises.

May the light of thy love shine on us this day,
    and bless our worship,
May we see a new glory in things we usually take for granted,
    and so be led to new rejoicing.
May we grow in the awareness of our world's opportunity
    and of our world's need, and so find a new calling
    in life.

May thy joy be in our hearts,
thy love be in our fellowship,
and thy glory be in and through everything we do this day.
For thine own name's sake we ask it.   AMEN

Readings: Genesis 1:27-31
Psalm 104:1, 10-15

Prayer of Thanksgiving
Wonderful are thy works O Lord God,
And we rejoice before thee in all the good things which thou
hast given us.
We rejoice that thou hast given us such a variety of trees
and plants to feed us,
And now we offer thee our thanks for them all.

For apples and oranges, bananas and pears,
and for all the fruit which grows on trees,
We thank thee O Lord.
For strawberries and raspberries, currants and brambles,
and for all the fruit which grows on bushes,
We thank thee O Lord.
For flowers and blossoms, and for all the beauty of spring
and autumn colours in the leaves,
We thank thee O Lord.
For potatoes and carrots, onions and turnips,
and all root crops,
We thank thee O Lord.
For farmers all over the world, for gardeners,
and for the scientists who serve them,
We thank thee O Lord.
For seamen, for railway staff, for lorry drivers,
and for all who work to bring us food from all over
the world,
We thank thee O Lord.
For people who work in shops and in vans,
especially those who serve us week by week,
We thank thee O Lord.
For those who cook our meals,
and for the joy we have in eating them,
We thank thee O Lord.
Yea Lord receive these our thanks for these and all thine
other mercies to us,
And grant us yet one thing more: grateful hearts to enjoy
thy Gifts.

And now
>> to the Father who gives every good and perfect gift,
>> to the Son, who died that we might live,
>> to the Spirit of love in our hearts,
Be glory and dominiion both now and for evermore,   AMEN

Hymn: 'Praise, O praise' (R.C.H. 620)

Readings: Deuteronomy 8:10-14, 17-18.
>> Psalm 65:1, 9-13.

Prayer of Confession
O Lord Our God,
We bless thee for all the wonders and joys of this world.
We bless thee for giving us such a large share in them.
We bless thee for thy Law, showing us how best to live in
this thy world.
But we confess that we have not lived as we should.

If we have eaten good food without giving thanks to thee,
>> Lord have mercy upon us, Christ have mercy upon us.

If we have taken for granted our high standard of living,
>> Lord have mercy upon us, Christ have mercy upon us.

If we have been concerned with sweets and ice cream while our
brothers and sisters lacked bread and water,
>> Lord have mercy upon us, Christ have mercy upon us.

If we have been anxious to get even more luxuries for ourselves rather than to give more help to those in need,
>> Lord have mercy upon us, Christ have mercy upon us.

If we have grumbled about what we have already, or have com-
plained that we have not more,
>> Lord have mercy upon us, Christ have mercy upon us.

If we have pampered our bodies with comforts and fancy foods
and have neglected to feed our souls with the bread of
heaven,
>> Lord have mercy upon us, Christ have mercy upon us.

If we have not spent our money in the way in which thou
wouldst have us spend it,
>> Lord have mercy upon us, Christ have mercy upon us.

If we have forgotten thee in our day-to-day living,
or have not lived according to thy laws of love,
>Lord have mercy upon us, Christ have mercy upon us.

We claim the promise of thy Word to all who are truly sorry
for having lived wrongly:
As for our transgressions, thou shalt purge them away . . .

Yea Lord, purge us from selfishness, greed and pride,
Purify our hearts from all that blinds us to thy presence,
so that we may indeed see thy hand at work in the world about
us, and rejoice in thy goodness.

Glory be to God our Father who has blessed us with all good
things,
Glory be to Christ, who suffered because of our sins,
Glory be to the Holy Spirit, who gives us new life,
To God, Father, Son and Holy Spirit be praise and glory
for ever,   AMEN

Hymn: 'Fountain of mercy, God of love' (R.C.H. 617)

Readings: Deuteronomy 24:19-22.
>Psalm 72:1-8

Prayer of Intercession
Blessed art thou, O Lord Our God, King of the universe, who
bringest forth food from the earth.
Blessed art thou, Jesus Christ, Lord of Lords and King of Kings,
for where thou reignest in the hearts of men hunger, poverty,
disease and injustice are thrown back.
Blessed art thou Spirit of God, Lord and giver of life,
teaching us to do the Father's will on earth.

Inspire us, and thy Church all over the world, to demonstrate
how to live in love for all men, that thy kingdom of justice
may be furthered, and all may see what is the Father's will
for his children.

Through the work of thy Church, O Lord:
>Thy kingdom come, thy will be done.

We pray for the rulers of the world,
For our own Queen and for her government,
For the work of the United Nations Food and Agricultural
Organisation.
> May the kingdoms of this world be more and more
> conformed to the pattern of thy kingdom, where men
> shall care for each other in brotherhood, as our
> Father wills.

Through the work of all peace-makers:
> Thy kingdom come, thy will be done.

We pray for all who work on farms and crofts, in gardens
and forests,
For those who gather the harvest of the seas,
And for those who work in mines,
And for all the scientists who serve and help them.

Through the toil of all these men and women:
> Thy kingdom come, thy will be done.

We pray for all who work in shops and in vans,
For those who transport our food by land, air and sea,
For those who process and distribute our food,
That they may see where their work fits into thy work of
providing for thy family, and know that thy will is guiding
them.

Through these by whose work we are fed:
> Thy kingdom come, thy will be done.

We pray for those who are hungry, or homeless,
For the sick, and for the sorrowful,
For all who receive the gifts we send out this day.
May the light of thy kingdom shine upon them even as we name
them before thee now in the silence of our hearts . . . . . .
For these, thy suffering children we pray:

> Thy kingdom come, thy will be done.

Now blessed be thy glorious name for ever,
Let the whole earth be filled with the glorious love

of our Father, in whom we are one,
of our Saviour who shares our sorrows and our griefs,
of our Holy Spirit of love and power, One God for ever,

AMEN

Hymn: 'Father, who on man dost shower' (R.C.H. 349)
Reading: Luke 12:15-21 (*read dramatically, the readers taking 'parts'*)

Offering

Prayer of Dedication
Here O Lord we lay before thee these gifts, the tokens of the greater offering of our lives in thy service.

We are thine for thou hast made us,
All that we have is thine already,
But now in love and gratitude we bring our offering to thee.

To thee we offer the work of farm and garden which has produced this harvest.
To thee we offer the skill and industry which has processed and distributed these thy gifts.
To thee we offer the work in our shops and vans, our buying and selling.
To thee we offer the work in our kitchens.
To thee we offer thy rightful place as head at our tables.

Since we draw our strength from the food which thou dost give us, we offer to thee our strength, O Lord.
Use us to further thy kingdom on earth.

And now, bind us together as one family,
brothers and sisters at thy table,
as together we pray:
OUR FATHER......

Hymn: 'We plough the fields' (R.C.H. 618)

Benediction

197

SECTION E

An Anthology of Prayers and Introductory Sentences

1

SENTENCES INTRODUCING WORSHIP

On All Occasions
We are glad to have this building to worship in. Its beauty delights us, its peace consoles us. But dearer to God than temples made with hands is the meeting together of his people.
Let us now join together in good spirit to worship the Lord our God, beginning with the prayer all Christians say:
OUR FATHER . . . . . .

On All Occasions
This first day of the week is the day when Jesus rose from the dead and became the living Lord.
That is why we gather here today as we do every Sunday.
Now is the time for us to celebrate God's grace and to draw new strength from Him whose presence is in the meeting together of his people.

On All Occasions
This week has brought to some joy and release, good fortune and an uplifted spirit.
To some it has brought anxiety, shock and sickness of heart.
To others again it has been a week of little note, with no disturbance of the routine round, either for good or ill.
How shall we join our hearts as one in worship today, we whose experience has been so different this week?
We shall remind ourselves that in Jesus Christ we are members one of another, to share each other's joys, to bear each other's burdens and to strengthen each other in the faith.

Harvest Festival

We are here today to celebrate a festival.
Today the church looks festal and smells fragrant with fruits
and flowers and vegetables of the earth.
It is our joy now to celebrate this festival and give voice
to the silent worship of beauty and abundance offered here
today.

All Saints

The community of faith is a wonderful fellowship.
It spans oceans and crosses frontiers. It embraces young and
old and reduces to nothing the line between time and eternity.
It is the bond by which all the faithful, here and hereafter,
are bound together in the one family of God's love through
Jesus our Lord.
We rejoice today to have part and share in this great com-
munion of saints.

Remembrance

With the passing of the years human memory grows dim, but
our faith is that lives forgotten and lost to us are not lost
to Almighty God.
Today in worship we are joining our remembrances with the
eternal remembrance of God.

Advent

The sacred year has revolved and today is a kind of new
year's day for us in the Church.
'He comes', we say, meaning the Lord Jesus Christ.
During this season of Advent we reflect how Christ is
constantly coming among us, day by day and week by week,
in the worship and fellowship of the Church.

Christmas Eve

Tonight when the world is at its darkest, the night its
coldest, a wonderful light and warmth is abroad in the hearts
and homes of men.
The Saviour says that except we become as little children
we miss his way for us.

Tonight we know the glory of simple faith.
Though it take us all life long to find again the trustful-
ness with which we were born, we know tonight that in such
faith lies our true peace.

New Year
The year has turned again and we are conscious that as time
passes our life is constantly changing.
But today we want to rejoice that our faith is in a God
whose grace is always ahead of us, so that we may meet life
as it comes to us not with fearfulness but with expectation.

Epiphany
At Epiphany we remember how Christ was visited and worshipp
by the Wise Men.
Wise though they were, they bowed in worship of a new-born
infant.
Though they were gentiles, they knelt before one who was born
a Jew.
All their fine gifts were offered to one who had scarcely
a roof over his head.
In the same spirit we offer our worship today in the knowledge
that before God there is none of us wise of simple, rich or
poor, Jew or gentile, but all are one in Christ Jesus.

Lent
These six weeks leading up to Easter are known as Lent, an
old name for Spring.
During these weeks we are leaving winter behind and looking
forward to the Church's own spring-time, the Resurrection.
Meanwhile, each Sunday is resurrection day as we share
together through worship in the risen life of Jesus.

Good Friday
Today is the saddest day of the Church's year, the day Jesus
was crucified.
Within the purpose of God, it seems, there must be this day
of darkness.

The Cross is a mystery, just as sorrow, sin and suffering are great mysteries in our own lives, but it is a mystery of grace and speaks of healing and consolation and peace.

Palm Sunday
On Palm Sunday we recall how our Lord entered the city while the people spread their garments in the way and cut down branches from the trees by way of welcome.
The children in the Temple shouted 'Hosanna', and even the very stones, it seemed, would cry out.
Let us now join our Palm Sunday praise with the Hosannas being sung today by Christian people everywhere.

Easter
How cheering it is to see the light of morning, to rise up to meet the rising day.
On such a morning, at Easter, at the fresh quiet hour of dawn, our Lord was alive from the dead.
Life has been the Christian theme ever since. Life is our theme today.

Ascension
We know that by descent we are dust of the ground but in the purpose of God we have an ascent as well as a descent.
God has set eternity within our hearts. Ours is the high calling of God in Christ Jesus.
Today as we remember the Ascension of our Lord let us remember that we also are ascended in him.

Whit Sunday
Today like the disciples of old we are wanting and waiting to receive God's good spirit.
We want him to fill our empty hearts. We need him to set our souls aflame.
As we join to worship with one accord let us lay ourselves open to the receiving of God's good spirit within our fellowship, through Jesus our Lord.

Trinity
We meet for worship today as we do each Sunday in the name of the Father, the Son and the Holy Spirit.

Through Jesus we worship God as him from whom cometh every good and perfect gift.
By him it is that anything in all creation should have being;
By him it is that grace and mercy should be flowing for the healing of our hurts?
By him it is that all these energies are ceaselessly poured forth.
Him we worship, Father, Son and Holy Spirit, one God blessed for ever.

2

CONTACT

*(After the singing of the opening hymn of praise
the congregation remain standing while taking part in this
dialogue.)*

Minister: Who are you?
Why have you come rejoicing and singing?
This is a fearful place: here you will meet your God.

People: We are men and women,
forgiven by Christ,
dedicated to Christ,
made brothers and sisters by him.
We have come to rejoice with song
For this is a joyful place: here we meet our Father.

Minister: Are you worthy to come here?
Have you been true followers of your Lord?

People: We stand here confessing our unfaithfulness,
acknowledging our unworthiness, but al
our potential, our commitment, our lov

Minister: Then let us pray with confidence and joy.

3

PRAYERS OF ADORATION

HOLY FATHER, our Creator and Sustainer, we worship
and praise you, for you have created ourselves and this world
from nothing.

We cannot understand the mystery of your kindness to us in
creation, but we acknowledge that we are not our own.

Your Love has overwhelmed us and humbled us.
Lord, we confess that we are not only unworthy of your
redeeming love, but we are unworthy of your creating love,
and so we thank you that you have given us life and time, and
by the Holy Scriptures instructed us that every good and
perfect gift comes from our heavenly Father.

LORD JESUS CHRIST, our Saviour and Lord, we worship
and praise you.
Our affections are roused as we gather today to remember your
death, and to share in its benefits.

You have loved us from before the foundation of the world,
and we have been given to you by the Father. We thank you
for your love and grace. We thank you that you are our
Good Shepherd, and know us each by name and by nature.

You have taken what is ours, that we might receive what is
yours.
You became poor that we might become rich.
You were announced on earth by lowly prophets that we might
be announced in heaven by glorious angels.
You were born into the kingdom of Herod that we might be
born anew into the kingdom of God.
You had nowhere to lay your head that we might possess the
place you have prepared for us.
You have tasted the cup of our woes and sorrows that we
might drink the cup of your fullness and joy.

You were silent before Pontius Pilate that we might have
your Name to speak before the judgement seat of God.
You wore a crown of thorns that we might wear a crown of
glory.
You reigned from a cross that we might reign from your
throne.
And you rose and ascended that now and at the last we might
be united to you in the presence of the Father.

Lord, how can we thank you enough? Only receive us we pray,
and draw near to us now, clothed in the garments of your
saving gospel.

HOLY SPIRIT, our Sanctifier and Strengthener, we worship
you.
You have shone brightly upon our Lord Jesus Christ, making
him visible to faith; you have shone into our hearts also,
dispelling our darkness and giving us faith to see and believe
in Jesus.

Help us we pray, to worship now with fervent and thankful
hearts, and, as you are the Spirit of Christ our Great High
Priest, and the leader of our worship, dwell amongst us,
leading us in our praise and worship, and preaching the
gospel to us from the Holy Scriptures.

FATHER, SON AND HOLY SPIRIT, gracious Trinity, we
bless and adore you; accept, sanctify, and enjoy all that we
are, all that we have, and all that we now offer to you,
because we ask it through the name of Jesus Christ our
Saviour and Lord, and for His glory,   AMEN

4

ADORATION AND MEDITATION

CHRIST ABOVE US: CHRIST BENEATH US:
CHRIST BESIDE US: CHRIST WITHIN US.
Invisible we see you, Christ above us.
With earthly eyes we see above us, clouds or sunshine,
grey or bright.
But with the eye of Faith, we know you reign:
> instinct in the sun ray,
> speaking in the storm,
> warming and moving all Creation, Christ above us.

We do not see all things subject unto you.
But we know that man is made to rise.
Already exalted, already honoured, even now our citizenship
is in heaven, Christ above us, invisible we see you.

Invisible we see you, Christ beneath us.
With earthly eyes we see beneath us stones and dust
and dross, fit subjects for the analyst's table.
But with the eye of faith, we know you uphold.
In you all things consist and hang together:
> The very atom is light energy,
> The grass is vibrant,
> The rocks pulsate.

All is in flux; turn but a stone and an angel moves.
Underneath are the everlasting arms.
Unknowable we know you, Christ beneath us.

Inapprehensible we know you, Christ beside us.
With earthly eyes we see men and women, exuberant or dull,
tall or small.
But with the eye of faith, we know you dwell in each.
You are imprisoned in the lecherous, the dope fiend and
the drunk, dark in the dungeon, but you are there.

You are released, resplendent, in the loving mother,
the dutiful daughter, the passionate bride,
and in every sacrificial soul.
Inapprehensible we know you, Christ beside us.

Intangible, we touch you, Christ within us.
With earthly eyes we see ourselves, dust of the dust, earth
of the earth; fit subject, at the last, for the analyst's
table. But with the eye of faith, we know ourselves all girt
about of eternal stuff,
> our minds capable of Divinity,
> our bodies groaning, waiting for the revealing,
> our souls redeemed, renewed.
Intangible we touch you, Christ within us.

Christ above us, beneath us, beside us, within us, what need
have we for temples made with hands? . . . save as a passing
place in which to gather and adore and be abased?
We are your living Temple, by Grace alone we are your living
body, the only hope of Clarity* for the world — Blessed
be your name for your glorious Gospel.

IT IS SO.

* Wyclif often uses the word Clarity for the word Glory.

5

A PRAYER OF APPROACH

Draw nigh, O God, in the quiet of worship. Hear and
receive our meditations both spoken and silently whispered
in the deep of our souls.

We come from so many different walks of life to gather here.
We bring with us joys and happinesses so great and so deep

that only you are capable of sounding them completely in our hearts. We bring with us sadnesses and griefs, anxieties and fears so terrible that we cannot even bring them to our lips in prayer, only trusting that your understanding is at work before words begin and where they cannot sound. We bring confusion, uncertainty and doubt . . . doubt about the meaning of life and about your purpose for our life. But, you are near, Father, very near, in the wonder of a single lifetime lived out upon our earth and in the Spirit of our Lord's victory. Here is the one event that makes sense of nonsense, wholeness of the broken, fragmented pieces of life. Here, indeed, is the true comfort, the only hope, the one peace, the perfect bond of love, the absolute assurance that death holds no sway over life, the promise that you are near.

In the light of your glory, Father, in the light of this love too great to comprehend, we are such unworthy creatures. We rant and rave upon our little stages. We grab and search for popularity, material wealth, position and status. Pride and petty-mindedness creep in. Jealousy warps our common sense. Like a terrible disease it drips venom in our hearts to poison all unselfish love, to chase away the last thought of obedience to your will. How easily we fall in weakness to temptation. Father, forgive us.

Instil in us a greater faith, a greater tenacity to the things we believe. When we doubt and are not sure, help our unbelief that our eyes may be opened and that our ears may hear, that our feet might follow the one who calls: 'I am the Resurrection and I am life. If a man has faith in me, even though he die, he shall come to life; and no one who is alive and has faith shall ever die.' Messiah, Son of God . . . we believe.   AMEN

6

PRAYER FOR THE RENEWAL OF THE CHURCH

Renew your church, O God,
beginning with me if you wish.

Renew your church, O God,
so that we may be better channels of your love.

Renew your church, O God,
so that bodies may be healed,
lives changed,
and all our lives bound more deeply together as brothers and
sister in Jesus Christ Our Lord.

7

A PRAYER FOR UNITY

Almighty God, you have made of one blood all the
nations of mankind so that we are all your children, and
members one of another. Why are we so slow to acknowledge yc
as our one Father? Our prayer, O God, is that you would make
the peoples one.

We pray for the Church of Christ so broken, scattered and
dismembered that none would think we followed one Lord and
held a common faith. Purge away the vanity, intolerance and
unforgiving spirit which keeps us far apart.

Our prayer is that since man's need is one we may all find
the one way to you, the one God. May the Spirit of Christ break
down all barriers and answer the desire of all nations. We
pray for a union so deep and universal that it shall gather
all within one fold . . . those who pray and those who cannot,
those whose faith is firm and those whose doubt is slow to
clear. May we never be content with anything that excludes
another from the fullness of your grace, a single soul from
the welcome of your heart.

Breath of God, Holy Spirit, as we seek you our God, enlighten
our hearts and our vision. As we turn to think of Jesus,
make our hearts to burn with love. Spirit of the living God,
Spirit of Christ, Spirit choosing the soul of man for your
dwelling, speak to us for we are ready to hear you.

8

EXCEPT THE LORD BUILD THE HOUSE . . .

O Jesus, Master Builder,
   as we work, day by day, on the house of life,
   may yours be the plans which we fulfil,
      yours the strength in which we work,
      yours be the specifications we work to,
      yours the oversight of each detail,
      and yours the glory when the scaffolding of the
      body is taken down at last, and the results of our
      labours are seen.
Unless it is you who are the real builder,
   we work in vain, O Lord.
On you we rely to provide us with all we need for our work.
May we find that we have built part of the Eternal City.

9

A GENERAL PRAYER

O Lord of triumph,
    you witness our defeat;
O God of victory,
    you sustain our failure;
O Father eternal,
    born in time —
make holy this time, that the love which was in Jesus may
be born in us,
    let the peace that passes understanding
    not pass us by,
Let us worship you.

God of heaven, you have called us your own, take us back
        from all the lonely places where we have strayed:
        from our personal failures lead us back to that place
        where we no longer accuse ourselves:
        from our sense of private emptiness lead us back to
        the fullness that is in you:
        from that blame, that regret, that remorse lead us
        back to a position of strength where we can once
        more love ourselves
            and our neighbour
            and our God, you most of all.

Here are words you may trust:
        Christ Jesus came into the world to save us, and of
        this we are now witnesses.
Father, we praise you for our new value which we did not earn,
we are glad to be here on a new road which we did not build:
Set our faces to the dawn, and let that dawn be now,
through Jesus Christ our Lord.   AMEN

10

A LITURGY OF INTERCESSION

(*For use in a house church or small street group*)

Let us pray
Let us bring to God the needs of his world, remembering
especially the people of this place, in their homes, in the
streets, and at their work.

We remember . . . . . . and . . . . . . and . . . . . .

Lord Christ, we uphold your people for mercy and for blessing
By your healing of the diseased
      (Reply) *Lord, heal the sick*
By your fortitude in the storm
      Lord, calm the fearful
By your fondness for little children
      Lord, protect the young
By your labour at a bench
      Lord, hallow our work
By your forgiveness on the cross
      Lord, pardon our sins
By your rising from the dead
      Lord, give us life

(*When this prayer comes at the end of an evening meeting,
it may be concluded thus:*)

And now, O God, in confidence we commit to you those whom
we love.
We commit . . . . . . and . . . . . . and . . . . . . (members not present)
We commit our families and our friends
We commit all those who come about our homes
We commit ourselves, and each the other.

May God the Father, God the Son, and God the Holy Spirit,
bless us and all those we love, this night and always.

11

A THANKSGIVING BY AFFLUENT CHRISTIANS

Father, we have many things which we treasure.
Day by day we have enough to eat, and we can pick and choose,
and eat what we like best.
We live in comfortable homes, well furnished, and well cared
for.
We own many useful things which make life easier, and delight-
ful things which make life more enjoyable.
Father, although some of us here have more than others, we
all have all that we need and more.
We want to say 'Thank you' now for all these good things:
and we want to say 'Thank you' for other things that make us
happy —
for the security and love of our homes and families,
for the company of our friends,
for work to do, and the skill to do it well,
for everything we have.

Father, it is easy to say 'Thank you';
it is harder to mean it.
Help us to be grateful every day for all that we have, and
for the comforts and joys of our life.
Help us to be grateful by reminding us again and again that
we have been given something better than all our possessions:
the life that Jesus lived among us.
In him we see the true face of God and the true face of man,
and without him, we would not know how to value anything we
have.
We do thank you, Father, for the life of Jesus, and we pray
that with the help of your Holy Spirit we may be able to show
our thankfulness in lives given to Jesus.
To him, and to the Spirit, and to you, our Father, we bring
our thanks, today and every day.   AMEN

12

THE MINISTRY OF RECONCILIATION

'God was, in Christ, reconciling the world to himself,
and he has committed to us the ministry of reconciliation'
2 Corinthians 5:19

O Christ, Great Reconciler of all men,
    inspire our prayers now,
    that as we pray, your love may radiate from us,
    continuing your work in us and through us.

Across the barriers that divide race from race, black from
white
    Reconcile us, O Christ, by your Cross.

Across the barriers that divide rich from poor,
starving from overfed,
    Reconcile us, O Christ, by your Cross.

Across the barriers that divide people of different religions,
atheists and believers,
    Reconcile us, O Christ, by your Cross.

Across the barriers that divide Christians of different
denominations, different theological outlooks,
    Reconcile us, O Christ, by your Cross.

Across the barriers that divide decent citizens from the
outcasts, the respectable from the down-and-outs,
    Reconcile us, O Christ, by your Cross.

Across the barriers that divide management from labour, office
staff from industrial workers,
    Reconcile us, O Christ, by your Cross.

Across the barriers that divide young and old, teenager and
middle-aged,
    Reconcile us, O Christ, by your Cross.

Confront us with the hidden prejudices and fears which deny
and betray the prayers we make outwardly.

Enable us to see the difference between the false sense of
superiority which causes strife, and the appreciation of what
contribution we do have to make.
May we grow in our sense of unity with all God's Children.

13

FOLLOWING A ROAD ACCIDENT

O Christ of the scarred and broken body,
  we hold up to you now, those who are injured . . . . . .
O Christ, as you share in earth's sorrows,
  we hold up to you now those who are plunged into
  sorrow . . . . . .
O Christ, as you carry the burden of the world's guilt,
  we hold up to you those who know that they were
  responsible . . . . . .
May your healing be upon each one of them.

And in the light of this we pray
  that we may never be responsible for causing an accident,
  that we may never bring such sorrow to others.
Help us to face the weaknesses in our own characters
  that might lead to disaster:
      the hunger for power,
      the suppressed anger,
      the desire to outdo other people.
And so save us from ourselves, O Saviour of Mankind.

14

CHRISTMAS

(*Based on Isaiah 9*)

Blessed be God who has given us new light!
Blessed be God that the darkness passes!
Blessed be God for the new day that breaks!

Jesus, Son of God, we welcome you,
   as you reveal the Father's love.
Jesus, Son of Man, we welcome you,
   as you bear the weight of our humanity.

O Jesus, Wonderful Counsellor,
   we who are puzzled, and who grope in the darkness our
   sins have made
      welcome you . . . give us light, Wonderful Counsellor.

O Jesus, Mighty God,
   we who are weakened by selfishness, and defeated by life,
      welcome you . . . rescue us, Mighty God!

O Jesus, Everlasting Father,
   we who have lost the sense of being God's family, his
   beloved,
      welcome you . . . bind us together in Love, Everlasting
      Father.

O Jesus, Prince of Peace,
   we who are weary of the wars that destroy our world
      welcome you . . . grant us your peace, Prince of Peace.

Spread your rule in our hearts,
and throughout the world,
until all men know who it is that is born in Bethlehem, and
who it is that works in our hearts, this day and for ever.

15

PRAYER FOR FUNERAL SERVICE

God we stand before you in the face of death. As it confronts us with its seeming finality, will you confront us with your certain eternity.

Help us to see death within the framework of your design of life. Help us to understand that having made man in your own image, you fashioned him for an eternal purpose and invested him with an infinite value which not even death can reduce.

Open our thoughts to perceive these truths that even now we may find peace, and healing, and strength. Through Jesus, our Lord,   AMEN

16

PRAYERS AFTER THE LESSONS AT A FUNERAL SERVICE

Eternal God, from whom we come, towards whom we go, and in whose sight all our lives are lived and every breath we draw is taken, we worship thee. We thank thee for the magnificent strength of our Christian faith, holding us at such a time as this. We thank thee for him who came to bear our burdens and carry our sorrows on the Cross before we ever have to bear them; who went down to the bottom of the pit of the human experience so that no man should ever be able to say 'God does not understand what that is like'; who rose

216

victorious over the grave robbing it of its power and sting,
and who has opened the kingdom of heaven to all who put their
trust in him.
We thank thee for the rod and staff upon which we can lean,
needing no other props; for a table spread in the midst of
all our adversities; the ability to say 'My cup runneth
over' in the midst of darkest grief; and for our sense of the
goodness and mercy which follow us all the days of our life
until we dwell in the house of the Lord for ever.

Father of mercy, and God whose very nature is compassion,
look in love and strength we pray thee upon this bereaved
family. Enable them to find in thee their refuge and their
strength, a very present help in trouble. Deliver them from
all doubt and bitterness, and help us to know that thou hast
prepared good things for those who love thee far beyond man's
understanding.

O thou before whose face the generations rise and pass, we
remember at a time like this all those in our intimate family
memory whose lives have been threaded with our own. And especially
this day we give thanks for the life of him/her whom thou hast
now taken to be with thyself. For every quality in his character
and every grace in his temperament, and everything he was as
a husband(?) and a parent(?) and a friend and a fellow human
being, we give thanks. . . . (*Special reference here if
necessary*) . . . And especially we thank thee that for him all
sickness and sorrow are over, and death itself is passed, and
we pray that his spirit may be in thy keeping in a peace and
beauty beyond all human imagining.

Bless O Lord, those nearest to him, who pick up the threads
of life from this day forward. Go where they go and abide
where they abide. Make a straight path for them amid all the
perplexities and loneliness of these days, and be their guide
and companion through them all. Forgive us all our sins, and
any way we wish we could undo the past and our abuse of days
that are gone; and in the days to come help us to live life
better and appreciate it more, in faith and hope and charity,

until for us the day comes when we are asked to give our life
back into thy hands. May it be that on that day we shall see
our loved ones again in heaven, and shall sing a new song
such as earth has never heard.

Glory be to the Father . . . . . .

17

ORDINATION

(Based on Isaiah 61)

The Spirit of the Lord our God anoint you with power
  to preach the Good News to the meek
  and the forgiveness of sins to the penitent
   in the name of Jesus.

The Spirit of the Lord our God anoint you with power
  to bind up the broken-hearted
  and to bring healing to the sick
   in the Name of Jesus.

The Spirit of the Lord our God anoint you with power
  to proclaim liberty to the captives of sin,
  and to challenge all who oppress the weak.

Faithful is he who calls you,
and faithfully will he work out what he has set out to
accomplish in you, and through you.

18
PRAYERS FOR THE PEOPLE WE MEET

May the light of faith burn brightly in us this week,
  so that those who are going through a difficult time
    may find encouragement through meeting us,
  so that those who are enjoying life may find their
    joy heightened by meeting us,
  so that those who are going wrong
    may find the challenge and help they need in
    meeting us.

May nothing in us prove a stumbling block to another's faith.
May nothing in us cause quarrels or strife.
May nothing in us cause pain to another.
O Light of the love of Christ, shine brightly in us, this
week, and for ever.

O Jesus, give us a deeper understanding of the people who
dislike us,
a purer joy in the people who love us,
and a greater power to help those who need us.

19
ABUNDANT LIFE

O Christ, you came so that we might have life, and have
it more abundantly,
  grant us power in our love,
  strength in our humility,
  purity in our zeal,
  kindness in our laughter,
  and your peace in our hearts at all times.

20
WHEN THERE IS A STRIKE

We pray for those involved in industrial strife:
>   For the Trade Union leaders,
>   For the representatives of management,
>   For the ordinary people who discuss the rights and
>   wrongs.
O Jesus, Lord of Justice and of Reconciliation, help us to
work out together what is best for our society.
>   Grant us strength to stand up for what is right,
>   without bitterness,
>   Grant us courage to admit where we are in the wrong,
>   without fear,
>   And grant us wisdom in all our discussions, that we
>   may say nothing that we will later regret.

21
EVENING

Abide with us, Lord,
>   for it is towards evening and the day is far
>   spent . . .
Abide with us, so that we, knowing your presence, may sleep
this night in the peace which the world can neither give nor
take away.

INDEX OF CONTRIBUTORS

SECTION A
1. Rev. James C. Stewart, St. Andrew's, Drumchapel.
2. Very Rev. Dr. Hugh O. Douglas, St. Mary's, Dundee.
3. Rev. Dr. T. Ralph Morton (Iona Community).
4. Rev. Ian Mactaggart, Craigmillar Park, Edinburgh.
5. Rev. Ian Pitt-Watson, New Kilpatrick, Bearsden.
6. Rev. A. Stewart Todd, St. Machar's Cathedral, Aberdeen.
7. Rev. Alan A. S. Reid, Old and St. Andrew's, Helensburgh.
8. Rev. Dr. W. A. Smellie, St. John the Baptist's, Perth.
9. Rev. A. Scott Hutchison, Rubislaw, Aberdeen.
10, 11. Rev. Wm. S. Whitson, Northfield, Aberdeen.

SECTION B
1. Rev. J. Stewart Miller, Mortlach and Cabrach.
2. Rev. W. John Harvey, Warden, Iona Abbey.
3. Rev. David S. M. Hamilton, West Church of St. Nicholas, Aberdeen.
4. Rev. Professor James A. Whyte, University of St. Andrews.
5. Rev. Ian Pitt-Watson, New Kilpatrick, Bearsden.
6. Rev. Professor William Barclay, University of Glasgow.
7. Rev. Professor David Cairns, University of Aberdeen.
9. Rev. David S. M. Hamilton, West Church of St. Nicholas, Aberdeen.
10. Very Rev. Lord MacLeod of Fuinary.
11. Mr. Stuart Harris, Slateford, Longstone, Edinburgh.
12. Rev. James C. Stewart, St. Andrew's, Drumchapel.
13. Rev. Professor James A. Whyte, University of St. Andrews.
14. Rev. J. L. Cowie, Richmond Craigmillar, Edinburgh.
15. Very Rev. Lord MacLeod of Fuinary.
16. Rev. Dr. Edmund S. P. Jones, Queen's Cross, Aberdeen.
17. Rev. Ian Clark, New Restalrig, Edinburgh.
18. Rev. A. Scott Hutchison, Rubislaw, Aberdeen.

SECTION C
1. Rev. Wm. S. Whitson, Northfield, Aberdeen.
2. Rev. T. H. Scott, Chaplain, Heriot-Watt University, Edinburgh.
3. Rev. Ian Clark, New Restalrig, Edinburgh.
4. Rev. Dr. T. Ralph Morton (Iona Community).
5. Iona Abbey Services.
6. Rev. David S. M. Hamilton, West Church of St. Nicholas, Aberdeen.
7. Rev. J. L. Cowie, Richmond Craigmillar, Edinburgh.
8. Rev. James C. Stewart, St. Andrew's, Drumchapel.

INDEX OF CONTRIBUTORS

SECTION D
1. Rev. David S. M. Hamilton, West Church of St. Nicholas, Aberdeen.
2. Rev. J. Stewart Miller, Mortlach and Cabrach.
3. Rev. J. L. Cowie, Richmond Craigmillar, Edinburgh.
4. Rev. Ian Pitt-Watson, New Kilpatrick, Bearsden.
5. Rev. W. Smellie, St. John the Baptist's, Perth.
6. Rev. David Ogston, Assistant, St. Giles' Cathedral, Edinburgh.
7. Mr. T. B. Honeyman, The Saint Andrew Press.
8. Mr. Stuart Harris, Slateford, Longstone, Edinburgh.
9. Rev. J. L. Cowie, Richmond Craigmillar, Edinburgh.
10. Rev. J. Stewart Miller, Mortlach and Cabrach.
11. Rev. Wm. S. Whitson, Northfield, Aberdeen.
12. Rev. David S. M. Hamilton, West Church of St. Nicholas, Aberdeen.
13. Rev. Ian L. Forrester, Inverkeillor, Arbroath.
14. Rev. David S. M. Hamilton, West Church of St. Nicholas, Aberdeen.
15, 16. Rev. Dr. Wm. Morris, Glasgow Cathedral.
17. Rev. J. L. Cowie, Richmond Craigmillar, Edinburgh.

SECTION E
1. Rev. J. H. McIndoe, St. Nicholas, Lanark.
2. Rev. Dr. Edmund S. P. Jones, Queen's Cross, Aberdeen.
3. Rev. Sinclair Ferguson, Assistant, St. George's Tron, Glasgow.
4. Very Rev. Lord MacLeod of Fuinary.
5. Rev. Wm. Hill, Kirkliston, West Lothian.
6. Rev. J. L. Cowie, Richmond Craigmillar, Edinburgh.
7. Rev. Wm. Hill, Kirkliston, West Lothian.
8. Rev. J. L. Cowie, Richmond Craigmillar, Edinburgh.
9. Rev. David Ogston, Assistant, St. Giles' Cathedral, Edinburgh.
10. Rev. W. John Harvey, Warden, Iona Abbey.
11. Rev. Wm. S. Whitson, Northfield, Aberdeen.
12, 13, 14. Rev. J. L. Cowie, Richmond Craigmillar, Edinburgh.
15. Rev. Tom Scott, Chaplain, Heriot-Watt University, Edinburgh.
16. Rev. Alan A. S. Reid, Old and St. Andrew's, Helensburgh.
17, 18, 19, 20, 21. Rev. J. L. Cowie, Richmond Craigmillar, Edinburgh.